Dimensions of a New Civilization

Exposure of Christian Treachery (Matt. 24: 5)

I0180981

ANDREW MASUKU

NEWCIVILIZATION.CO.ZW
HARARE, ZIMBABWE

Original Cover Design: [AnkoZim Digital Studio (Pvt)Ltd]
Book Layout ©2013 BookDesignTemplates.com

Ordering Information:
Quantity sales; Special discounts are available on quantity pur-
chases by corporations, and others. For details, contact
www.lightiningsource.com, or www.ingramspark.com
Dimensions of a New Civilization/Andrew Masuku – 1st edition. ISBN: 978-0-7974-6672-2

DEDICATION

This Book is dedicated to my mother, Mrs Meggie Masuku (nee Mbano), aged 89 in the year 2015. She exuded enthusiasm for God's word. Translation into Sindebele and Shona languages was considered--to also benefit those in similar circumstances.

ACKNOWLEDGMENTS

I am indebted to some Christian friends who gave their generous objective impressions and technical support. However, I withhold mentioning names to skirt the risk of omitting others along the way; taking comfort in that it is God who rewards all labours of love.

Those who, for one reason or another, could not submit comments are also appreciated, as their prayers count. Though bearing the author's name, I consider this book to be a collective effort among those who desire to spread the gospel of Jesus Christ.

My wife, Faith, and children are also appreciated for their patience and tolerance. Even though they might not have fully comprehended my commitment to this project; out of love, they limited possible interruptions to the barest minimum. But my special tribute goes to my son, Arnold, to whom I feel indebted for his experience in book publishing.

While appreciating regular insightful literature from Grace Communion International (www.gci.org), this work is solely the Author's responsibility, without necessarily reflecting the views of GCI. Over and above everything, I give glory to God. The inspiration to write could not have come through any other way, except through God's empowering Spirit.

FOREWORD BY ROBERT KLYNSMITH

I found this book certainly interesting, insightful and thought-provoking; well-written, and a good read, with core elements of Christianity beautifully woven, and revealing God's unconditional love for humanity.

My feedback is primarily focused on the general rather than specifics, bearing in mind there are so many different schools of thought about theology and matters of doctrine. I suppose we will all be surprised at how much we did not know or understand when Christ returns. As Paul says, we see through a glass, darkly.

CONTENTS

Copyright...ii
Dedication iii
Acknowledgments...iv
Foreword..v
Preface..vi
1. Causative Framework of Christianity............................14
2. Flesh and Sinfulness...18
3. Who is Jesus?..23
4. The Distinction between "Son of Man" and Son of God........28
5. Two Contrasting representations of Jesus...................33
6. Mystery in Man's Creation..37
7. The Magnificent and Mysterious Third Heaven...........41
8. The Prodigal Son and God's Kingdom..........................46
9. Is There Life Beyond the Physical?..............................49
10. Resurrection and Judgment...52
11. The Seven-Day Week and the Sabbath.......................57
12. Miracles and parables...62
13. Personal Salvation vs. God's Kingdom.......................66
14 . Forget About Mineral Resources................................70
15. The Delusions of Introversion.....................................75
16. Poverty and Wealth...80
17. Happiness Comes from Making Others Happy...........85
18. Safety Precautions..89
19. Seven Obstacles of Christian Faith............................93
20. Seven Attributes of Abraham......................................98
21. Earthy Parents are Mere Custodians 103
22. Fellowship with focus..108
23. Idolatry: The Worship of Self and False gods...........114
24. Christians Should Not Avoid Confronting the Spirits........119
25. Christianity and Family Members..............................123
26. Church Leadership...128
27. Church Financing...134
28. Prayer and God's Will..140
29. True Christianity...145
30. The Significance of the Great Commission...............150

31. Exploring the Concept of the Trinity..154
32. The Brotherhood of Humanity..159
33. Deducing the Truth: A Path to Freedom................................163
34. Like Jesus, Every Individual is born with a mission...........167
35. The Most Perilous Risk in Christianity..................................171
Glossary...176
Bibliography...186

PREFACE

According to the Judeo-Christian Bible, the mission of Jesus Christ was to reverse the negative effects of human civilization. This book explores the profound impact of two contrasting philosophical concepts: self-centeredness and altruism. It invites readers to reflect on the ultimate purpose of their lives and the legacy they leave behind.

The mission of this book is twofold:
To help readers discover new insights rooted in Scripture and invite constructive dialogue, in addressing inconsistencies between this work and Biblical facts. This book is written with candour, aiming to analyze Christian faith in a way that deepens understanding and inspires action toward God's Kingdom.

Its thirty-five chapters address common misunderstandings and present biblical teachings as practical tools for fostering meaningful relationships and transforming lives. The story of Jesus' sacrifice serves as the ultimate standard, offering a blueprint for replacing the broken systems of our world with a New Civilization founded on love and responsibility.

Love is central to Christianity, yet it remains one of the most misunderstood and misapplied concepts in human history. True love is not merely an emotion but a way of life—a commitment to adding value to others, as demonstrated by Jesus in His words, actions, and relationships. The New Civilization calls for full responsibility, where individuals become agents of positive change, illuminating the world like a beam of light dispelling darkness.

This book upholds the principle of being our brother's and sister's keeper. It emphasizes understanding the root causes of conflict before addressing animosities, paving the way for reconciliation and excellence in relationships. It is written for those who hunger and thirst for righteousness—those willing to study the Bible with the diligence of a student, seeking wisdom until their last breath.

No one possesses a monopoly on wisdom or knowledge. True enlightenment lies in attentive listening, thoughtful evaluation, and the humility to learn from others, regardless of their background or education. Wisdom is reflected in the ability to recognize folly, even in oneself, and to grow from it. Humanity's interconnectedness means that our lives are shaped by the wisdom—or folly—of those around us. Thus, the pursuit of wisdom is a shared journey.

At the heart of this book is Jesus Christ, who unveils the mysteries of God's Kingdom. As the Scriptures exhort, *"Prove all things; hold fast to what is good"* (1 Thessalonians 5:21, KJV). This calls for careful listening and discernment (Proverbs 18:13), ensuring that readers are firmly rooted in their faith rather than swayed by every passing doctrine. Biblical teachings must be evaluated against the life and words of Jesus, not merely the interpretations of others.

While this book reflects my personal convictions, I avoid dogmatism, recognizing that knowledge is infinite and our understanding is always evolving. Readers are encouraged to revisit this book, as one would a revelatory data, to uncover deeper insights and identify any areas where the text may fall short of the divine standard found in God's Word. I welcome constructive feedback and open to dialogue, as I too am on a journey of growth and learning.

A Christian author is not infallible, nor inherently superior to the reader. Only the Bible stands as the inspired and authoritative guide for those seeking God's Kingdom. If you resonate with this affirmation, we share a common fellowship, transcending denominational boundaries. For those eager to explore these teachings further, I am available to engage in meaningful discussion and mutual edification.

To aid understanding, a glossary is included at the end of the book, clarifying key terms and phrases used throughout. My hope is that readers will approach this book with an open mind and heart, ready to be challenged, inspired, and transformed.

May those reading be richly blessed as they embark on this journey of discovery.
Andrew Masuku
May 9, 2015

The Christian Bible is used as stable datum, with the following versions used interchangeably:

The New International Version (NIV) Thomson Chain Reference Bible: 1982 Edition

King James Version (KJV) (Thomas Nelson, Inc.) 1989 Edition

English Standard Version (ESV) (Crossway Bibles) 2001 Edition

American Standard Version (ASV) www.e-Sword.net – Rick Meyers 2010 Edition

English Majority Text Version (EMTV) www.e-Sword.net – Rick Meyers 2010 Edition

1965 Bible in Basic English (BBE) www.e-sword.net – Rick Meyers 2010 Edition

English Standard Version (ESV)

`

CHAPTER 1

CAUSATIVE FRAMEWORK OF
CHRISTIANITY

I was inspired to write after observing many Christians who seem to overlook the profound significance of Christian doctrines. Why does one belong to a particular church group? Is it due to a genuine conversion, or simply the result of cultural upbringing? Christianity demands more than mere social affiliation.

It calls for a commitment to principles that transcend ordinary human gatherings. While belonging to a group is part of Christianity, it comes with added responsibilities that require a transformation in behaviour: *"Therefore, if anyone is in Christ, he is a new creation; the old has gone, the new has come"* (2 Corinthians 5:17, NIV).

True Christians renounce their share in the current civilization, which is often marked by fleeting pleasures and empty smiles. *"We know that the whole creation has been groaning as in the pains of childbirth right up to the present time. Not only so, but we, who have the first fruits of the Spirit, groan inwardly as we wait eagerly for our adoption as sons, the redemption of our bodies"* (Romans 8:22-23, NIV).

The media daily amplifies stories of despair, yet offers no real solutions. Corruption permeates every sphere of society. Political upheavals, dictatorships, and systemic injustices plague the lives of ordinary people. This vicious cycle persists as long as individuals believe they have no alternative for rational survival.

Compounding these issues are global terrorism, xenophobic attacks, the proliferation of illicit drugs, and the normalization of immoral behaviour. Wickedness has become socially acceptable, and even human rights activism is sometimes questioned due to the pervasive influence of self-centeredness.

Diseases, natural disasters, and untimely deaths leave countless children orphaned and even adults broken, confined to psychiatric asylums. The weight of such evil drives some to despair, even to the point of suicide, rather than face the overwhelming miseries of this broken world.

It is true that some profit from the current state of civilization—funeral undertakers, drug dealers, security agents, arms dealers, and even the media. Their survival interests, combined with the general populace's complicity in immoral behaviour, perpetuate and exacerbate these unacceptable conditions.

While Africa may appear to bear the brunt of these issues due to rampant self-centeredness, the problems affecting one part of humanity inevitably spread to others, transcending social, racial, political, and economic boundaries.

The betterment of human society is the responsibility of those who, though ill-equipped, desire survival. Most people sense that something is profoundly wrong. If there was ever a time to replace this civilization, it has always been now. God's plan of redemption, fulfilled through Jesus Christ, offers the only true path to survival.

Christians, called out of sin, are tasked with spreading the gospel, whose doctrine is rooted in altruism. Even criminals can be used to preach the gospel. Is this to demonstrate that God's truths apply to all, regardless of their past? Or is it to highlight the unconditional nature of His redemptive plan?

Jesus personally mentored twelve disciples, chosen not for their intellectual prowess or social standing, but for their willingness to follow Him. These ordinary individuals, often seen as unsophisticated, were entrusted with the mission of advancing the gospel. They were expected to transcend their differences and cultivate a culture of love, embodying the principles of the New Civilization.

The temptations Jesus faced validated His mission and identity (Matthew 4:4-10). Satan, who had ensnared Adam and plunged humanity into spiritual paralysis, sought to thwart Jesus' redemptive mission. Yet, Jesus overcame where Adam failed, confirming His Messiah-ship and fulfilling His divine purpose.

Jesus' divine love required Him to identify with sinners, becoming the perfect sacrifice for their redemption. God's love, manifested in human form, brought light to those groping in the darkness of sin.

As Jesus travelled through Galilee and surrounding regions, many accepted Him, but those in His hometown rejected Him. His reading of the prophetic scroll in Nazareth, which confirmed His Messiah-ship, incited anger (Luke 4:18-24). The Jews expected a conquering Messiah, not one who preached love and forgiveness. They could not comprehend a kingdom founded on love rather than power.

God's Kingdom is eternal because it is built on love, not hatred. In contrast, earthly kingdoms are established by vanquishing enemies, leaving a legacy of resentment. Jesus' method of loving one's enemies remains a radical and often misunderstood concept.

Loving one's enemies does not mean condoning sin. Jesus' love calls sinners to repentance, offering redemption to those who accept it. Those who reject this offer face the consequences of their choice.

The miracles Jesus performed—healing the sick, giving sight to the blind, and cleansing lepers—drew crowds and demonstrated His divine authority. Yet, His popularity incited envy and anxiety among religious leaders, who feared losing their influence.

Jesus' mission was to replicate His love and power in His followers. *"Very truly I tell you, whoever believes in me will do the works I have been doing, and they will do even greater things than these"* (John 14:12, NIV). His goal was to multiply His presence through those who faithfully applied His principles.

In three and a half years, Jesus upended religious norms, performing unprecedented miracles and revealing the principles of God's Kingdom. He redefined leadership by serving others, even washing His disciples' feet (John 13:4-15). This act symbolized the inversion of power structures in the New Civilization, where leaders serve rather than dominate.

The New Civilization challenges the status quo, calling for love instead of hatred, service instead of domination. It is heroic to love one's enemies and pray for their deliverance (Matthew 5:44), a stark contrast to the world's values.

The danger in preaching the gospel lies not in failure but in success, which can breed pride. Jesus warned, *"Not everyone who says to me, 'Lord, Lord,' will enter the kingdom of heaven, but only the one who does the will of my Father"* (Matthew 7:21, NIV). Those who boast of their achievements risk hearing, *"I never knew you. Away from me, you evildoers!"* (Matthew 7:23, NIV).

Salvation is not earned by works but received by grace through faith (Ephesians 2:8-9). No one can boast before God, for even the greatest achievements are gifts from Him. The Wise Men from the East and the conversion of Paul illustrate that God can use anyone, even those outside the faith, to accomplish His purposes.

The foundation of Christianity is Christ, the cornerstone of salvation (Isaiah 28:16). Those who trust in Him need not fear failure, for His grace is sufficient. *"For it is by grace you have been saved, through faith—and this is not from yourselves, it is the gift of God—not by works, so that no one can boast"* (Ephesians 2:8-9, NIV).

The New Civilization calls for a rejection of self-centeredness and an embrace of altruism. It is a radical shift from the world's values, offering hope, restoration, and the promise of eternal life. Through Christ, we find the power to transform relationships, overcome evil, and live in the light of God's Kingdom

---

CHAPTER 2

FLESH AND SINFULNESS

When a rich young ruler addressed Jesus as "Good Master," Jesus' response challenged a long-held misconception (Matthew 19:16-17, KJV). Though Jesus lived a perfect life in the flesh, He clarified that His physical nature, in itself, was not inherently good. Jesus existed in a dual reality: fully human and fully divine.

For thirty-three and a half years, He walked the earth, embodying our physical nature, yet His life represented the Kingdom of God—a civilization entirely distinct from our own. The term "Christ" signifies the prophesied Messiah, unseen by human eyes but existing in the eternal divine order.

Jesus, in His humanity, represented our sinful state, while as Christ, He embodied our redemption. The Jews failed to recognize this duality, leading them to reject their Messiah. They could not reconcile the humble, human Jesus with their expectations of a conquering king.

When a person dies, their physical body decomposes and must be disposed of—whether through burial or cremation. Only the good works they leave behind endure.

A lifeless body is no different from compost. Life, as we understand it, is sustained by breath and blood circulation. Yet, humanity's greatest error is its obsession with the desires of the flesh—temporary and sinful pursuits that hold no eternal value.

The flesh is perishable; it returns to dust. Only the spirit is imperishable. Life and death are opposites, just as flesh and spirit are opposites. Adam became a living soul only after God breathed life into him (Genesis 2:7).

But after the departure of life, the body decays, leaving nothing of value. God told Adam, "Dust you are, and to dust you shall return" (Genesis 3:19). This was the consequence of sin—a forfeiture of the divine life God had given.

The physical body is sustained by the intricate workings of the brain, but it is the spirit that gives life. "The Spirit gives life; the flesh counts for nothing" (John 6:63, NIV). Confusion arises when we assume the physical body controls life, rather than the other way around. This misunderstanding lies at the heart of humanity's struggles. Christ came to address this confusion and restore our understanding of true life.

"So I say, live by the Spirit, and you will not gratify the desires of the sinful nature. For the sinful nature desires what is contrary to the Spirit, and the Spirit what is contrary to the sinful nature. They are in conflict with each other, so that you do not do what you want" (Galatians 5:16-17, NIV).

The devil perpetuates the lie that the physical body is the essence of human existence. But a spiritual being does not need a physical body to survive. It is the body, destined for the grave that depends on the life-giving Spirit.

Humanity is sustained by three components: the spirit, the soul, and the body. The soul, governed by the mind, chooses between the flesh and the spirit. The spirit aligns with Godly principles, while the flesh craves sin.

When we say, "My conscience tells me this is wrong," it is the spirit speaking. The flesh has no conscience. When the flesh dominates, the spirit is weakened, leading to degradation. The spirit within us, distinct from the Holy Spirit, guides us toward life (Job 32:8). Its power is magnified when united with the Holy Spirit (Romans 8:16).

Christ provides access to the Holy Spirit, which leads to life. Those who listen to the spirit, rather than the flesh, often face humiliation, persecution, or even death. Yet, in their physical suffering, their spirit grows stronger. The battle between flesh and spirit is won or lost through the will-power—choosing between sin and death or righteousness and life. Consider the temptation of adultery.

19

The flesh rationalizes indulgence, while the spirit whispers, "This is wrong." Succumbing to the flesh weakens the spirit, leading to habitual sin and its consequences— broken relationships, disease, or even death. Conversely, heeding the spirit preserves life. Adultery is just one example; the flesh craves many forms of sin (Galatians 5:19-21).

Overcoming these desires is not easy. The allure of sin leads to death, a curse inherited from Adam. But through Christ, we can crucify the flesh and its lusts (Galatians 5:24-25). Life is found in the spirit, while death is the result of yielding to the flesh.

Sacrifice is necessary to reject the pleasures of sin and follow the spirit. "Whoever finds their life will lose it, and whoever loses their life for my sake will find it" (Matthew 10:39, NIV). This paradoxical truth calls us to choose between the temporary desires of the flesh and the eternal life offered by the Spirit.

The flesh and the spirit cannot coexist peacefully. One must be sacrificed for the other. The flesh is temporary and corruptible; the spirit is eternal. Choosing the spirit requires intellectual and spiritual resolve. It means surrendering the fleeting pleasures of the flesh to discover the eternal life Christ offers.

In protecting the flesh and denying Christ's power, we lose eternal life. Our mortal bodies will perish, but in Christ, we defeat death (1 Corinthians 15:55-57). The flesh's only lasting value is its return to the earth. Its temporary nature is starkly illustrated by Zimbabwe's life expectancy in 2009— which was 37 years for men and 34 for women. Such statistics remind us of the fragility of physical life.

Yet, even in our brief physical existence, we can choose to leave a legacy of good works. Jesus' 33½ years on earth profoundly impacted humanity because He submitted entirely to God's will. We, too, can use our time to build character and serve others, leaving the world better than we found it.

As Roy Bennett[1] wrote, *"When you die, you will take neither wealth nor prestige with you, but you can surely leave the world a worse place than it was. Or a better place. It is the daily, sometimes small, choices that make for a life and a legacy. What will yours be?"*

The early church provides an example in Dorcas (Tabitha), whose good works for widows and the poor led to her miraculous resurrection (Acts 9:36-42). Through Christ, death is defeated, and eternal life is assured for those who align with His will.

Jesus declared, "Man does not live on bread alone, but on every word that comes from the mouth of God" (Matthew 4:4, NIV). His physical survival depended not on food or shelter but on obedience to God. Even in His suffering on the cross, Jesus prioritized the eternal over the physical. His resurrection demonstrated that life is not confined to the flesh.

Paul reminds us, "Therefore, brothers and sisters, we have an obligation—but it is not to the flesh, to live according to it. For if you live according to the flesh, you will die; but if by the Spirit you put to death the misdeeds of the body, you will live" (Romans 8:12-13, NIV). As children of God, we are heirs with Christ, called to share in His sufferings and glory.

Ultimately, the physical nature is temporary, but the spirit is eternal. By prioritizing the spirit over the flesh, we align ourselves with God's Kingdom and the promise of eternal life.

End Notes

1. Roy Bennett, "Smoke and Mirrors: Another look at politics and ethnicity in Zimbabwe" from the text of the speech at Rhodes House, Oxford, freezimbabwe.com May 29, 2012

[Flesh And Sinfulness]

CHAPTER 3

WHO IS JESUS?

To declare that another human being is Jesus might invite scorn, especially from those accustomed to viewing Jesus through the lens of the Trinity. Yet, when Jesus came to bring light, humanity often chose to remain in the comfort of confusion.

"Then the righteous will answer him, saying, 'Lord, when did we see you hungry and feed you, or thirsty and give you drink? And when did we see you a stranger and welcome you, or naked and clothe you? And when did we see you sick or in prison and visit you?' And the king will answer them, 'Truly, I say to you, as you did it to one of the least of these my brothers, you did it to me'" (Matthew 25:37-40, ESV).

The identity of Jesus cannot be fully grasped through theological studies alone. True understanding comes through divine revelation. Jesus came directly from God to demonstrate the significance of godliness.

The only distinction between Jesus and humanity is that Jesus possessed full knowledge of God's Kingdom— knowledge that remains inaccessible to the world
Jesus is "the way, the truth, and the life" (John 14:6).

He is the model for how to live a life that pleases God. True Christians are called to reflect Jesus, not to worship Him as an idol. During His earthly ministry, Jesus never sought worship. Instead, He taught His disciples the principle of servant-hood.

Before His crucifixion, He washed their feet to illustrate this truth (John 13:1-17). Though His disciples regarded Him as Lord, Jesus never instructed them to worship Him. He directed them to pray to the Father, not to Himself.

The doctrine of the Trinity, while widely accepted, is not explicitly sustained by Scripture. It represents human attempts to explain divine mysteries, often unnecessarily complicating the simplicity of God's nature.

God cannot be likened to anything physical. Genesis tells us that humanity was created in God's image, yet physical humans cannot fully represent God's divine nature. As John wrote, "If anyone says, 'I love God,' and hates his brother, he is a liar; for he who does not love his brother whom he has seen cannot love God whom he has not seen" (1 John 4:20).

The incarnation of God was most profoundly revealed in Jesus. Yet, this incarnation extends to all humanity through His resurrection. To reject another human being is to reject God; to love another is to love God. Before Jesus, humanity struggled to understand God's nature. Jesus clarified this through His life and teachings.

The terms "Father," "Son," and "Holy Spirit" describe different aspects of God's relationship with humanity. Jesus used these terms to explain the process of spiritual transformation. For example, access to the Father is only through Jesus, and the Holy Spirit seals believers as children of God.

No human language can fully capture God's divinity, which transcends all creation. Christians are called to rely on Jesus' teachings as the ultimate truth (John 14:6).

In the expression "Jesus Christ," the name "Jesus" is personal, while "Christ" is a title. "Jesus" is the Greek form of the Hebrew "Joshua," meaning "Jehovah is salvation." The name "Jesus" connects Him to humanity, not divinity. The confusion arises when we idolize Jesus' humanity rather than emulate His example.

The name "Jesus" itself carries no divine connotation, as seen in Hebrew Scripture. Below are seven characteristics of the man Jesus that highlight His humanity:

1. **Jesus as the Son of God**: While Jesus is the Son of God, so are all humans, created in God's image (Genesis 1:26). His humanity made Him unidentifiable, even to the point of being betrayed by Judas' kiss.

2. **Jesus as the Son of Man**: Jesus often referred to Himself as the "Son of Man," identifying with humanity and representing us in His crucifixion.

3. **Jesus' Humanity**: Jesus refused to be called "good Master" (Matthew 19:17), emphasizing that His humanity was not to be idolized.
4. **Jesus' Anguish on the Cross**: On the cross, Jesus cried, "My God, my God, why have you forsaken me?" (Matthew 27:46). This was the cry of a human in agony, not a divine being.
5. **Jesus' Physical Limitations**: As a human, Jesus experienced pain and prayed as we do. God, being Spirit, does not suffer physically.
6. **Jesus' Mission**: Jesus sought not to be served but to serve (Matthew 20:28). Though divine, He related to us in our humanity.
7. **Jesus' Teachings**: Respecting Jesus' humanity means loving others as He commanded (Matthew 25:44-45; 1 John 4:20).

The name "Jesus" reflects His humanity, while His divine nature is revealed in Isaiah's prophecy: "For to us a child is born, to us a son is given... and his name shall be called Wonderful Counsellor, Mighty God, Everlasting Father, Prince of Peace" (Isaiah 9:6, ESV).

Jesus' humanity and divinity are inseparable. Through Him, God took on human form to save humanity (Hebrews 2:14-18). On the cross, Jesus bore our sins and endured mockery on our behalf (Luke 23:35-37). His sacrifice fulfilled His mission of reconciling humanity to God.

Jesus' identity is further revealed in His teachings. He said, "I am the way, and the truth, and the life. No one comes to the Father except through me" (John 14:6 ESV). To accept Jesus as Saviour is to emulate His life and teachings, as the apostle Paul explained:

"Have this mind among yourselves, which is yours in Christ Jesus, who, though he was in the form of God, did not count equality with God a thing to be grasped, but emptied himself, by taking the form of a servant, being born in the likeness of men" (Philippians 2:5-7 ESV).

The parable of the prodigal son (Luke 15:11-32) beautifully illustrates God's love and justice. The father's unconditional welcome of the wayward son mirrors God's boundless grace, while the elder son's bitterness reflects the struggle experienced by Jesus on the cross—a dynamic that parallels the rejection Jesus faced, even as He bore the punishment we deserved.

The story of Jesus encapsulates Christ's sacrificial love, offering us reconciliation with the Father. Jesus' authority and mission are further affirmed in His declaration: *"All authority in heaven and on earth has been given to me. Go therefore and make disciples of all nations..."* (Matthew 28:18-20, ESV).

The term "Christian" was first used in Antioch to describe Jesus' followers (Acts 11:26). However, true discipleship is not about labels but about embodying Jesus' teachings. Paul urged believers to be "all things to all people" (1 Corinthians 9:22), emphasizing actions over titles.

Jesus represents the ideal human, created in God's image. Instead of distancing ourselves from His humanity, we are called to identify with it. As John wrote, "Whoever loves God must also love his brother" (1 John 4:21).

Ultimately, Jesus' humanity and divinity reveal the mystery of God's Kingdom incorporation in physical humans. By emulating His life, we participate in the New Civilization He inaugurated—a world transformed by love, humility, and service.

CHAPTER 4

THE DISTINCTION BETWEEN "SON OF MAN" AND "SON OF GOD"

The confusion between the titles "Son of Man" and "Son of God" lies at the heart of much misunderstanding in Christianity. This confusion not only contributed to the crucifixion of Jesus but continues to obscure the true nature of His identity.

A proper understanding of these terms is essential for spiritual clarity. Truly converted individuals are guided to move beyond this confusion and embrace Jesus as the Son of the living God. While Christians recognize Jesus as the Son of God, His consistent self-identification as the Son of Man reveals a deeper, often overlooked truth.

The Biblical Foundation

In Matthew 16:13-20, Jesus asks His disciples, *"Who do people say the Son of Man is?"* They respond with various opinions: John the Baptist, Elijah, Jeremiah, or one of the prophets. Jesus then turns the question to them:
"But what about you? Who do you say I am?" Simon Peter answers, *"You are the Christ, the Son of the living God."* Jesus affirms Peter's revelation, stating that it was divinely inspired. However, He then warns His disciples not to tell anyone that He is the Christ. This passage raises three critical questions:

- *Why did Jesus ask this question specifically to His disciples?*
- *Why did He frame the question in terms of the "Son of Man" rather than the "Son of God"?*
- *Why did He instruct His disciples to keep His identity as the Christ, a secret?*

28

Unveiling the Mystery

Jesus sought to reveal a profound mystery to His disciples. Despite clear prophecies about the coming of the Messiah, the world failed to recognize humanity's divine identity as children of God. Jesus' miraculous virgin birth and the announcement by the Wise Men were extraordinary events, yet even the religious scholars of His time could not grasp their significance.

For example, in Isaiah 7:14, the prophecy of the virgin birth was given: *"Therefore the Lord himself will give you a sign: The virgin will conceive and give birth to a son, and will call him Immanuel."* Yet, when this prophecy was fulfilled in Jesus, many failed to recognize Him as the promised Messiah.

Jesus referred to Himself as the "Son of Man," a title that set Him apart. Ordinary people do not typically call themselves "sons of men." This unique self-designation underscores His humanity while pointing to His divine mission.

Though accused of claiming to be the Son of God, Jesus consistently identified Himself as the Son of Man, emphasizing His connection to humanity. He walked among people as one of them. He also hinted at His future return as the Son of Man (Matthew 24:44; Acts 1:11).

The Son of Man in Prophecy

Scripture foretells the Son of Man's appearance in glory and power. Matthew 24:30 states, *"At that time the sign of the Son of Man will appear in the sky, and all the nations of the earth will mourn. They will see the Son of Man coming on the clouds of the sky, with power and great glory."*

This imagery contrasts with the unseen nature of the Son of God, who is revealed only to His disciples. The world cannot see the Son of God, but the Son of Man's return will be visible to all.

For instance, in Daniel 7:13-14, the prophet describes a vision of the Son of Man: *"In my vision at night I looked, and there before me was one like a son of man, coming with the clouds of heaven. He approached the Ancient of Days and was led into his presence. He was given authority, glory, and sovereign power; all nations and peoples of every language worshiped him."*

This prophecy aligns with Jesus' description of His return, emphasizing His role as the divine ruler who will establish an everlasting kingdom.

The Sons of God and the Daughters of Men

Genesis 6:1-3 highlights the distinction between the *"sons of God"* and the *"daughters of men."* This passage reveals a spiritual separation caused by the intermingling of divine and human lineages. God's Spirit could not contend with humanity indefinitely because of this corruption.

The crux of the matter lies in the danger of seeking divine son-ship while still identifying as a *"son of man."* This duality leads to spiritual confusion and blasphemy, as warned in Exodus 20:7 and Matthew 12:31.

For example, in 2 Corinthians 6:14-18, Paul warns against being "unequally yoked" with unbelievers, emphasizing the need for spiritual separation. This principle echoes the distinction between the sons of God and the daughters of men, highlighting the importance of maintaining a pure relationship with God.

The Parabolic Teaching of Jesus

Jesus often taught in parables to shield unconverted individuals from the full weight of divine truth (Mark 4:10). The term "Son of Man" was a fitting descriptor for His earthly ministry, as it resonated with humanity's understanding. However, the deeper truth of His identity as the Son of God was reserved for those who were spiritually prepared to receive it.

For instance, in Matthew 13:10-13, Jesus explains to His disciples why He speaks in parables: *"Because the knowledge of the secrets of the kingdom of heaven has been given to you, but not to them."* This approach ensured that only those with open hearts and minds could grasp the deeper spiritual truths.

The Tree of Life and Redemption

The banishment of Adam from the Garden of Eden (Genesis 3:22-24) symbolizes humanity's separation from eternal life. Access to the Tree of Life was barred to prevent eternal existence in a state of sin. Jesus' redemptive work restored humanity's access to this divine life, fulfilling the prophecies of old. His teachings, often shrouded in parables, safeguarded humanity from prematurely accessing the Holy Spirit before conversion.

For example, in Revelation 2:7, Jesus promises, *"To the one who is victorious, I will give the right to eat from the tree of life, which is in the paradise of God."* This promise reflects the restoration of humanity's access to eternal life through Christ's sacrifice.

Alienation from the World

Jesus, as the Son of the living God, was not of this world. His followers, too, experience this alienation, often facing persecution and scorn (Matthew 5:10-12). Authentic Christianity is marked by a willingness to stand apart from worldly approval. As 1 John 4:5-6 explains, those who are of God listen to His truth, while the world listens to its own.

For instance, in John 15:18-19, Jesus warns His disciples, *"If the world hates you, keep in mind that it hated me first. If you belonged to the world, it would love you as its own. As it is, you do not belong to the world, but I have chosen you out of the world."* This passage underscores the inherent tension between the values of the world and the calling of Christ's followers.

The Danger of Group Identity

Humanity's tendency to seek belonging in groups often leads to spiritual compromise. Whether through racial, tribal, or religious identities, people cling to collective norms for security. However, true spirituality transcends these boundaries. Each individual is uniquely created in God's image, with a distinct purpose. Just as the body's parts serve different functions, each person contributes to the whole without superiority or inferiority.

For example, in 1 Corinthians 12:12-27, Paul uses the analogy of the body to describe the church: *"Just as a body, though one, has many parts, but all its many parts form one body, so it is with Christ."* This passage emphasizes the importance of diversity and unity within the body of Christ, rejecting the notion of hierarchy based on worldly standards.

Conclusion

Jesus came as the Son of Man to bridge the gap between humanity and divinity. His earthly ministry, death, and resurrection fulfilled prophecies and revealed humanity's potential for redemption. The distinction between the Son of Man and the Son of God is crucial for understanding Jesus' mission and our own identity as children of God. By embracing this truth, we move beyond confusion and into the fullness of divine revelation.

CHAPTER 5

THE TWO CONTRASTING
REPRESENTATIONS OF JESUS

I n Christianity, discerning between falsehood and truth is of
paramount importance. Jesus Christ is the central figure of
Christianity, and His name holds profound significance.
However, in these last days, Satan exploits the name of Jesus,
presenting counterfeit versions of Christ that appear attractive
but are designed to deceive. These counterfeits aim to lead
people away from the genuine Jesus, the Savior of humanity.

The Warning about Deception

Jesus Himself warned about the rise of false Christs
and false prophets. In Matthew 24:5 (KJV), He said, *"For many
shall come in my name, saying, I am Christ; and shall deceive
many."* These deceivers know how to use Jesus' name to mis-
lead people, presenting a distorted version of Him that appeals
to human desires but ultimately leads away from the truth.

Similarly, in Matthew 7:15 (ESV), Jesus cautioned,
*"Beware of false prophets, who come to you in sheep's clothing
but inwardly are ravenous wolves."*

Outwardly, these deceivers may appear righteous and
harmless, but their true nature is destructive. Today, countless
individuals and groups claim to represent Jesus, but not all are
genuine. It is crucial to distinguish between the counterfeit
Christ used for deception and the true Christ who delivers humanity.

The Humble Appearance of Jesus

The genuine Jesus, as described in the Bible, was born
in humble circumstances. He was born to Mary in Bethlehem

of Judea, but grew up in Nazareth, a town associated with poverty and obscurity. His appearance was ordinary, indistinguishable from the poor people of His time. Yet, His being was extraordinary, for He was God incarnate.

For example, in Matthew 26:47-50, Judas Iscariot had to use a kiss to identify Jesus to those who sought to arrest Him. This indicates that Jesus did not stand out physically; He looked like any other ordinary person. His parents, Joseph and Mary, were not religious elites or Temple officials. Joseph was a carpenter, a humble profession that likely left little time for elaborate religious rituals.

Despite this, some today portray Jesus' birth and upbringing as extraordinary, elevating Mary to a status of sainthood that is not supported by Scripture. Artistic depictions often show Mary as a highly revered figure, but the Bible presents her as an ordinary woman who faithfully followed God's laws.

Even Jesus, at one point, seemed to downplay His familial ties, emphasizing spiritual kinship over biological relationships. In Matthew 12:49-50 (NIV), He said, *"Here are my mother and my brothers. For whoever does the will of my Father in heaven is my brother and sister and mother."*

The Misunderstood Jesus

The Jesus of the Bible does not align with the popular image many Christians hold today. The prophet Isaiah described Him in Isaiah 53:2-3 (ESV):
"He had no form of majesty that we should look at Him, and no beauty that we should desire Him. He was despised and rejected by men, a man of sorrows and acquainted with grief."
This description contrasts sharply with the majestic, radiant figure often depicted in art and media.

If Jesus were to appear today as Isaiah described, many Christians might struggle to recognize or accept Him. They might even reject Him, just as the religious leaders of His time did.

For instance, Nicodemus, a Pharisee, visited Jesus at night, likely to avoid being seen with someone considered disreputable (John 3:1-2). Today, many might similarly distance themselves from a Jesus who does not fit their expectations of holiness and grandeur.

The Deception of False Prophets

Satan's strategy is to present a counterfeit Jesus who appeals to human pride and desires. False prophets often promise blessings, prosperity, and comfort, focusing on what people can receive rather than what they are called to give. This distorted message attracts many, but it leads them away from the true Gospel.

For example, in Luke 14:25-34, Jesus made it clear that following Him requires sacrifice and self-denial. He warned that those who seek to be His disciples must be willing to give up everything. Yet, many today are drawn to preachers who promise wealth and success, ignoring the call to take up their cross and follow Him.

The True Jesus: A Life of Giving

The genuine Jesus is not focused on receiving but on giving. He taught that it is more blessed to give than to receive (Acts 20:35). His life was marked by service, sacrifice, and love for others, even those who rejected Him. He associated with sinners, tax collectors, and the outcasts of society, seeking to bring them hope and redemption.

In Matthew 11:19, Jesus was criticized as *"a friend of tax collectors and sinners."* He did not seek the approval of the religious elite or the admiration of the crowds. Instead, He focused on adding value to the lives of those in need. This self-less love stands in stark contrast to the pride and self-interest that often characterize false prophets.

The Danger of Pride

Pride is one of Satan's most effective tools for deception. It appeals to our desire for recognition, respect, and admiration. Many are drawn to leaders who exude confidence, charisma, and success, but these traits can mask a ravenous wolf in sheep's clothing.

For instance, in 1 John 2:16, the Bible warns against "the pride of life," which is not from God but from the world. Pride leads us to focus on ourselves rather than on God and others. It blinds us to the truth and makes us vulnerable to deception.

The Call to True Discipleship

True Christianity is not about receiving blessings but about giving ourselves to others. It is about following the example of Jesus, who *"came not to be served but to serve, and to give His life as a ransom for many"* (Matthew 20:28). This requires humility, selflessness, and a willingness to be misunderstood or even rejected.

In Matthew 5:10-12, Jesus said, *"Blessed are those who are persecuted for righteousness' sake, for theirs is the kingdom of heaven."* True discipleship often involves suffering and sacrifice, but it also brings the joy of knowing we are following in the footsteps of our Savior.

Conclusion

The two contrasting representations of Jesus—the counterfeit and the genuine—reveal the importance of discernment in Christianity. The counterfeit Jesus appeals to our desires for comfort, recognition, and prosperity, but He leads us away from the truth. The genuine Jesus calls us to a life of humility, service, and sacrifice, offering us the true riches of His Kingdom.

By focusing on giving rather than receiving, we align ourselves with the true Christ and resist the deception of false prophets. Let us strive to know the real Jesus, the man of sorrows who gave His life for us, and follow Him with all our hearts.

CHAPTER 6

MYSTERY IN MAN'S CREATION

The creation narrative in Genesis holds profound mysteries that, without careful examination, leave humanity in confusion. To clarify the distinction between the creation of *Man* in God's image (Genesis 1:26-27) and the formation of *Adam* from dust (Genesis 2:7), the following thirteen-point analysis provides a digestible framework:

1. **God's Image is Spiritual:** God's image is inherently spiritual. Anything physical, including humanity's corporeal form, stands in contrast to this spiritual reality.

2. **Adam's Physical Form**: Adam's formation from dust (Genesis 2:7) is distinct from the creation of Man in God's image (Genesis 1:26-27). Adam's loneliness and vulnerability to deception highlight his separation from the divine image. The NIV Thomson Reference Bible (1982) footnote suggests Adam is not synonymous with the Man of Genesis 1:26-27.

3. **Goodness in Creation:** The declaration that creation was "very good" (Genesis 1:31) includes the Man in God's image, not Adam, who fell to Satan's deception.

4. **Adam's Corporeal Nature:** God's statement, *"Dust you are, and to dust you will return"* (Genesis 3:19, NIV), underscores Adam's inferiority to the spiritual *Man* created in God's image.

5. **Jesus as the "Son of Man":** When the Gospels refer to Jesus as the "Son of Man," they point to the Man in God's image, infused in the earthly Adam. Jesus embodies the divine image of humanity that ought to have been the case before sinning.

6. **Paul's Distinction:** Paul contrasts the earthly man (Adam) with the heavenly man (Jesus): *"As was the man of dust, so are those who are of the dust; and as is the man of heaven, so are those who are of heaven. Just as we have borne the image of the man of dust, we shall also bear the image of the man of heaven"* (1 Corinthians 15:48-49, BBE).

7. **Temporary vs. Eternal:** Material things are temporary, but the spiritual is eternal. *"We fix our eyes not on what is seen, but on what is unseen. For what is seen is temporary, but what is unseen is eternal"* (2 Corinthians 4:18, NIV).

8. **The Corpse and the Spirit:** A corpse is merely a body; the true self is the spirit created in God's image. Christ's sacrifice liberated humanity from the prison of physicality.

9. **Christ's Temple:** Jesus declared, *"Destroy this temple, and in three days I will raise it up"* (John 2:19). His body was the temple, but His reality was not the temple itself. Crucifying His body did not destroy His divine nature.

10. **Jeremiah's Calling:** God told Jeremiah, *"Before I formed you in the womb I knew you, before you were born I set you apart"* (Jeremiah 1:5, NIV). This reveals that God's knowledge of humanity precedes physical formation.

11. **Corporeal vs. Spiritual:** The need for food and survival (Genesis 1:28-29) highlights humanity's corporeal nature, which contrasts with the spiritual image of God.

12. **Obsession with the Physical:** Obsession with physical survival blinds us against spiritual reality. After death, the unconverted cannot expect union with God, after their physical nature decays.

13. **Jesus' Mission:** Jesus restores humanity to God's image. Adam's genealogy does not reflect this image, but Jesus does (2 Corinthians 4:4; Colossians 1:15; Hebrews 1:3).

The creation story culminates in the Man created in God's image—the pinnacle of God's "very good" creation (Genesis 1:27, 31). This divine image reflects God's perfection, as embodied in Jesus. However, if God does not need food for survival, neither ought the Man in His image.

God creates something from nothing, but humanity, formed from dust, creates nothing from something—often destroying life for survival. The Adamic man represents a flawed groundwork for developing godly character. Loving one's enemies, for example, mirrors God's nature by creating the goodness from evil.

Humanity's mismanagement of the earth has led to global crises, such as climate change and natural disasters. These are consequences of the Adamic nature, not the *Man* in God's image. Adam's lineage threatens creation, necessitating its removal for restoration.

Adam's formation from dust (Genesis 2:7) contrasts with the spiritual creation of *Man* in Genesis 1:26-27. The dust represents a temporary, physical state, while the divine image is eternal. Understanding this distinction is crucial for spiritual growth.

The physical product mirrors an artist's concept of what would be real. Destroying the physical product does not necessarily destroy the concept. Similarly, the physical nature is temporary, although representing the reality, while the spiritual nature is eternal and real. Humanity often mistakes the physical for reality and the spiritual for illusion.

Jesus, as the *"image of the invisible God"* (Colossians 1:15), embodies the divine image described in Genesis 1:27. He is the prophesied Messiah who reveals God's nature to humanity. By identifying with Jesus, we renounce Adam's genealogy and embrace our true identity as children of God.

Adam's need for a helper (Eve) attracted his downfall. In contrast, the *Man* in God's image needs no helper, as he is one with God. Jesus, the *"Son of Man,"* validates this identity, calling us to reject Adamic attributes and embrace our divine heritage.

The Tree of Knowledge of Good and Evil symbolizes humanity's fall into sin. God's plan of redemption, fulfilled through Jesus, restores access to the Tree of Life (Revelation

22:14). Satan, like Judas, played a role in this plan, unwittingly advancing God's purpose.

Physical existence is a training ground for developing godly character. Through trials and suffering, we learn dependence on God. Jesus' sacrifice offers redemption, breaking the curse of Adam's lineage and restoring humanity to God's image.

To renounce Adam's genealogy is to embrace Jesus' attributes. This requires faith and a willingness to let go of cultural and sinful dictates. Jesus' mission is to restore humanity to perfection, offering salvation through His grace.

Fear of death stems from a lack of faith in Christ's victory. Baptism symbolizes death to the old self and resurrection to new life in Christ (Romans 6:4-9). Through Him, we overcome the fear of death and embrace eternal life.

The New Civilization, rooted in Jesus, calls us to live as the *Man* created in God's image. By rejecting the Adamic nature and embracing Christ, we participate in God's eternal plan of redemption for humanity

THE MAGNIFICENT
THIRD HEAVEN

Heaven stands in stark contrast to the earthly realm. Yet, to avoid speculation, it is essential to define heaven clearly, grounding our understanding in Scripture rather than human imagination. Although Jesus is not physically present to guide us, the Holy Scriptures provide the direction we need. The Apostle Paul's description of the three heavens offers a framework for comprehending the heaven Christians aspire to attain.

"I know a man in Christ who fourteen years ago was caught up to the third heaven. Whether it was in the body or out of the body I do not know—God knows. And I know that this man— whether in the body or apart from the body I do not know, but God knows—was caught up to paradise and heard inexpressible things, things that no one is permitted to tell" (2 Corinthians 12:2-4 NIV).

From an earthly perspective, the first heaven is often understood as the sky—the visible expanse where birds fly. The second heaven is the celestial realm where stars and planets reside. The third heaven, however, is the dwelling place of God, a realm beyond human comprehension.

Trinitarian advocates often depict it as inaccessible to ordinary humanity, and indeed, the mysteries of God are beyond our natural understanding.

Yet, Paul, a human like us, claimed to have been taken up to the third heaven fourteen years prior to writing this letter. This event coincided with his conversion to Christianity. Once a persecutor of Christians,

Paul's transformation began on the road to Damascus, where he intended to continue his campaign against the followers of Jesus. It was there that he experienced the divine encounter he later described to the Corinthians.

"As he neared Damascus on his journey, suddenly a light from heaven flashed around him. He fell to the ground and heard a voice say to him, 'Saul, Saul, why do you persecute me?' 'Who are you, Lord?' Saul asked. 'I am Jesus, whom you are persecuting,' he replied. 'Now get up and go into the city, and you will be told what you must do'" (Acts 9:3-6 NIV).

The third heaven is not an exclusive experience reserved for Paul alone. It remains accessible to all apostles and believers. Being caught up in the third heaven is not a unique privilege but a profound spiritual encounter that true Christians may share. This experience transforms their behaviour, setting them apart from the world. Christianity, at its core, is not a complicated religion—it simply requires a willingness to be guided by Scripture.

The first group of Christians to experience the third heaven comprised the eleven apostles and others present on the Day of Pentecost, as described in Acts 2. Jesus had promised them this spiritual ascent, assuring them of their union with Him. While Paul's encounter occurred on the road to Damascus, the apostles experienced it collectively on Pentecost.

"I will not leave you as orphans; I will come to you. Before long, the world will not see me anymore, but you will see me. Because I live, you also will live. On that day you will realize that I am in my Father, and you are in me, and I am in you. Whoever has my commands and keeps them is the one who loves me. The one who loves me will be loved by my Father, and I too will love them and show myself to them" (John 14:18-21 NIV).

This passage challenges Trinitarian views, as Jesus promises His disciples that they will join Him in paradise, within their lifetimes. This aligns with His statement that those who follow His teachings will not experience death (John

8:51). In Jesus' view, physical death is not the end but a transition.

A common human struggle is the understanding of the nature of death. The Christian narrative reveals that life is deeply connected to its source. Plants draw life from the earth, fish from the water, and terrestrial beings from the air.

Just as a plant withers when uprooted or a fish perishes out of water, humans cannot thrive without their connection to God. Adam, formed from dust, was sustained by the earth and its produce. Yet, his disobedience severed this divine connection, leading to spiritual death.

"Then the Lord God said, 'Behold, the man has become like one of Us, to know good and evil. And now, lest he put out his hand and take also of the tree of life, and eat, and live forever'— therefore the Lord God sent him out of the garden of Eden to till the ground from which he was taken" (Genesis 3:22-24 NKJV).

Adam's banishment from Eden symbolizes humanity's separation from divine joy. This story, though symbolic, communicates a profound truth: our disconnection from God is the root of spiritual death. The journey back to God requires transformation, a process often marked by trials and challenges.

Jesus addressed this spiritual death directly, offering a path to restoration. When He told a would-be follower, *"Let the dead bury their own dead, but you go and preach the kingdom of God"* (Luke 9:60 NKJV), He was emphasizing the priority of spiritual life over earthly obligations. To become a child of God is to transcend earthly ties and reclaim the paradise lost by Adam.

This is the same paradise Paul described. True Christians, though perceived as ordinary in this world, reside in this spiritual realm. The moment one becomes a child of God, they enter paradise and are freed from the fear of death. This truth, however, is incomprehensible to the world, as Jesus noted. To declare oneself in paradise is to invite misunderstanding, even ridicule.

Jesus' unity with the Father was a central theme of His ministry and the cause of His crucifixion. The Jews, misunderstanding His divine nature, accused Him of blasphemy. Yet, Jesus affirmed His identity, citing Scripture:

"Is it not written in your law, 'I said, "You are gods"'? If He called them gods, to whom the word of God came, do you say of Him whom the Father sanctified and sent into the world, 'You are blaspheming,' because I said, 'I am the Son of God'?" (John 10:34-36 NKJV).

This passage reveals the danger of pride and ignorance. Those who lack understanding often react emotionally, clinging to false beliefs to protect their egos. Jesus' resurrection exposed their error, affirming His divine authority.

For Christians, Jesus is the ultimate standard. Each believer is accountable to God individually, free from the hierarchies and traditions that often misguide. As Jesus taught, *"Do not be called 'Rabbi'; for One is your Teacher, the Christ, and you are all brethren. Do not call anyone on earth your father; for One is your Father, He who is in heaven"* (Matthew 23:8-9 NKJV).

In God's household, there is no hierarchy. Every believer, regardless of gender or status, is a child of God. As Paul wrote, *"You are all sons of God through faith in Christ Jesus"* (Galatians 3:26 NKJV). The diversity of roles within the body of Christ reflects the harmony of God's design, not a ranking of importance.

Paradise, then, is not a distant corner of the universe but a spiritual reality within the believer. It is the indwelling of God, experienced at baptism when one is united with the Father, Son, and Holy Spirit. From that moment, the believer is no longer of this world but a citizen of heaven.

"Now, therefore, you are no longer strangers and foreigners, but fellow citizens with the saints and members of the household of God, having been built on the foundation of the apostles and prophets, Jesus Christ Himself being the chief cornerstone" (Ephesians 2:19-20 NKJV).

This is the paradise Paul described—a spiritual realm where God dwells within His children. The physical body of a

[The Magnificent Third Heaven]

Christian is God's dwelling place, or a Temple, according to Paul (1 Corinthians 6:19-20). It is not a future hope but a present reality for those who have embraced faith in Christ.

CHAPTER 8

THE PRODIGAL SON AND GOD'S KINGDOM

The parable of the prodigal son (Luke 15:11-32) has been preached for centuries, often highlighting the themes of repentance and forgiveness. While it draws parallels between those who stray from faith and those who remain steadfast, Jesus' use of this parable carries a deeper, more profound significance.

It reveals the mystery of humanity's relationship with God and the eternal bond between the Father and His children. At its core, the parable reflects the perpetual relationship between Jesus and His Father—a bond that transcends human understanding.

In human terms, a father-son relationship often involves a deep, enduring connection. Even in our physical condition, after a father's death, a son may strive to fulfil his father's dreams.

However, human relationships are limited by their physical nature, ending at death. Infidelity, misunderstandings, and other complications further obscure these bonds.

Yet, humanity's true origin is not earthly but divine. Physical existence is temporary, but our spiritual identity is eternal. When Jesus instructed His disciples, *"Call no man your father on earth, for you have one Father, who is in heaven"* (Matthew 23:9, ESV), He was emphasizing this spiritual reality.

God, who declared, *"Let us create man in our image"* (Genesis 1:26), is humanity's true Father. Despite this, humanity often resists this truth, clinging to earthly identities and relationships.

Jesus' teachings, often delivered in parables, reveal deeper spiritual truths to those who seek understanding. As He explained to His disciples,

"To you has been given the secret of the kingdom of God, but for those outside, everything is in parables, so that 'they may indeed see but not perceive, and may indeed hear but not understand, lest they should turn and be forgiven'" (Mark 4 10-12, ESV).

These mysteries were not meant for casual listeners but for those willing to forsake everything to follow Christ, as Peter and the disciples did (Matthew 19:27).

The parable of the prodigal son (Luke 15:11-32) serves as a profound allegory for humanity's relationship with God. The father's unconditional love for his wayward son mirrors God's boundless grace toward sinful humanity, offering forgiveness and restoration to those who return to Him.

Meanwhile, the elder son's expression of bitterness and resentment ought to be understood in the context of physical humanity. It reflects the struggle with self-righteousness, paralleling the anguish Jesus endured on the cross.

In bearing the punishment humanity deserved, Jesus made reconciliation with the Father possible, bridging the gap between a broken world and a loving God. The elder son's grievances—feeling overlooked despite his faithfulness— mirror Jesus' cry on the cross: *"My God, my God, why have you forsaken me?"* (Matthew 27:46, ESV).

Just as the father assured the elder son, *"You are always with me, and all that is mine is yours"* (Luke 15:31, ESV), mirrors God's affirmation of Jesus' authority over humanity. Hence, after His resurrection, Jesus declared, *"All authority in heaven and on earth has been given to me"* (Matthew 28:18, ESV).

The parable underscores the sacrificial love of Jesus, our brother, representing what was foreshadowed in Moses' prophesy, *"The Lord your God will raise up for you a prophet like me from among you, from your brothers—it is to him you shall listen"* (Deuteronomy 18:15, ESV).

Jesus, though sinless, bore the sins of humanity, fulfilling the role of the sacrificial lamb. Although faithful, the elder son felt neglected by his father. His obedience to the Father's will, even unto death, exemplify the selfless love and service expected of God's children.

The prodigal son's return symbolizes humanity's redemption, celebrated by the Father with joy. Yet, the elder son's struggle highlights the cost of faithfulness. Jesus' suffering on the cross seemed like a momentary forsaking by the Father, but it was ultimately a demonstration of divine love and justice.

Through His resurrection, Jesus claimed all authority, assuring His followers of their eternal inheritance. Christianity, therefore, is not limited to earning God's favour but also about embracing our identity as His children. It involves surrendering our will to His, just as Jesus did, for us to reconnect as God's children.

The Holy Spirit empowers believers to overcome challenges and live in alignment with God's will. As Jesus said, *"I am the way, and the truth, and the life"* (John 14:6, ESV), He invites us to follow His example and share in His lordship.

The parable of the prodigal son ultimately reveals God's desire for a perpetual relationship with humanity. It challenges us to move beyond temporary, earthly attachments and embrace our eternal identity as God's children.

While the idea of eternal life may seem abstract or even unappealing to some, it is the fulfilment of our divine purpose. God, in His love, grants us the choice: to accept eternal life with Him or to reject it.

CHAPTER 9

IS THERE LIFE BEYOND
THE PHYSICAL?

The concept of life after death is one of the most misunderstood and debated topics, often leading to confusion among Christians and non-Christians alike. Many theories have been proposed, but few align with the biblical truth.

A common belief is that the righteous go to heaven while the unrighteous suffer eternal torment in hell. While this idea may motivate repentance, it often fosters a self-centred mindset rather than the altruistic love that Christ exemplified.

The resurrection of the dead is as certain as the rising sun tomorrow. The hope of our salvation and resurrection are more real than our physical current existence. Our salvation rests on faith in this promise, not on our works. Faith is sustained by understanding, based on the belief in Jesus having shown the way to life. As Paul writes:

"Now if Christ is proclaimed as raised from the dead, how can some of you say that there is no resurrection of the dead? But if there is no resurrection of the dead, then not even Christ has been raised. And if Christ has not been raised, then our preaching is in vain and your faith is in vain... If in Christ we have hope in this life only, we are of all people most to be pitied" (1 Corinthians 15:12-19, ESV).

Revelation 20 outlines the events surrounding Christ's second coming and the establishment of His eternal Kingdom. To interpret Scripture correctly, we must always view it through the lens of Christ's role as our Saviour. As the only way towards our salvation, humanity is doomed without Jesus, who comes again to be observed in physical form.

At His return, Christ will execute divine justice, but not in the way humanity expects. His justice is rooted in love, not vengeance. At Gethsemane, Jesus rebuked Peter for attempting to defend Him with a sword, saying, *"Put your sword back into its place... for all who take the sword will perish by the sword"* (Matthew 26:52, ESV).

Peter's reaction reflected the world's mindset, but Jesus revealed a higher way: defeating evil with good, hatred with love, and darkness with light.

Satan, the deceiver of nations, will be bound for a thousand years, before a New Civilization is ushered (Revelation 20:1-3). During this time, peace and righteousness will prevail. However, after the millennium, Satan will be released to test humanity once more. Those who have known only God's Kingdom will face the choice between good and evil, just as Adam did in Eden.

The first resurrection involves the saints—those who have remained faithful to Christ, even through trials and persecution (Revelation 20:4-6). These saints will reign with Christ, serving as celestial beings, but appearing in physical form to guide and teach those still living in their physical lives on earth.

Like Christ, the saints will manifest physically to interact with humanity, yet remain celestial. Ordinary humans will still need to have to choose to renounce their physical bodies, for them to also be embraced in God's Kingdom. Jesus' appearance presents the greatest opportunity for humanity to experience the essence of God's truth.

Not all who call themselves Christians will necessarily be part of this first resurrection. Some, though outwardly religious, will be disappointed to find they have not truly known Christ. Jesus warned, *"Not everyone who says to me, 'Lord, Lord,' will enter the kingdom of heaven, but only the one who does the will of my Father who is in heaven"* (Matthew 7:21, NIV).

The parable of the ten virgins (Matthew 25:1-13) illustrates the importance of spiritual preparedness. The wise virgins, who kept their lamps filled with oil (symbolizing the Holy Spirit), were ready for the bridegroom's arrival. The foolish ones, unprepared, were left outside. Similarly, Christians must remain vigilant, filled with the Spirit, to be ready for Christ's return.

The parable of the net (Matthew 13:47-50) further emphasizes the separation of the faithful Christians against the unfaithful ones. Just as fishermen sort good fish from bad, Christ will separate those who truly belong to Him from those who do not.

The depicted sifting concerns those chosen among millions of Christians, but not yet the judgment that comes after the millennium. In other words, those false Christians, although disappointed, will not be condemned yet.

For those having failed to qualify, there will still be hope in them, as long as having been caught still alive at Jesus' second coming. During Christ's millennial reign, they will have another opportunity to embrace God's truth and possibly receive salvation. However, those who persist in rebellion will face the second death—eternal separation from God (Revelation 20:14).

The disappointment of pseudo-Christians at Christ's return will be profound. Like the Pharisee in Jesus' parable (Luke 18:9-14), they may have relied on their own righteousness rather than God's grace. Pride blinds them to their need for a Saviour, leading to frustration and despair.

Ultimately, life beyond the physical is a reality confirmed by Christ's resurrection. Those who belong to Him will inherit eternal life, free from the limitations of flesh and blood. As Paul writes, *"Flesh and blood cannot inherit the kingdom of God, nor does the perishable inherit the imperishable"* (1 Corinthians 15:50, NIV).

The New Civilization, established by Christ, will be marked by love, justice, and peace. It is a Kingdom where self-centeredness is replaced by altruism, and where God's will is done on earth as it is in heaven. The millennial reign of Christ does not include those having died before the second coming of Jesus, except for the resurrected Saints.

CHAPTER 10

RESURRECTION AND JUDGMENT

The concept of resurrection and judgment is central to understanding God's plan for humanity. Jesus taught that in the resurrection, people will live like angels, neither marrying nor being given in marriage (Matthew 22:29-32). This state describes the saints, who will reign with Christ in the first resurrection (Revelation 20:6).

The second resurrection, coming after the millennium, is for judgment, not necessarily for acquiring eternal life, for some people (Revelation 20:13). During the Great White Throne Judgment, the dead will be resurrected in physical form, although their lives will no longer follow the patterns of their former existence.

Just as Christians today are called to live transformed lives after conversion, those resurrected at this judgment will face a transition toward eternal life—or eternal separation from God.

"For it is time for judgment to begin with God's household; and if it begins with us, what will the outcome be for those who do not obey the gospel of God?" (1 Peter 4:17, NIV).

The Great White Throne Judgment focuses on those having died before the second coming of Jesus. This includes some of those identified as Christians, but having not been part of the first resurrection. As depicted in Matthew 25:32-46, the entire humanity having ever lived in this world since Adam, faces judgment. These individuals, being resurrected for judgment, at that time, fall into three categories:

First Category: Those Who Never Heard the Gospel

This group includes people who died without hearing the gospel or who showed no interest in it. They span all of human history, from Adam to the present day, including many Israelites who lived before Christ. While some, like the Israelites, may have been familiar with God's promises, most will encounter the gospel for the first time at this judgment.

Old Testament prophecies, such as Isaiah 65 and Ezekiel 37, provide insight into this period. Isaiah speaks of a time when God will reveal Himself to those who did not seek Him (Isaiah 65:1). Ezekiel's vision of dry bones coming to life symbolizes a physical resurrection, not the spiritual reality of God's Kingdom (Ezekiel 37:1-14). The spirit beings do not have bones, describing physical humans.

These individuals will have the opportunity to understand and accept God's truth, just as those encountering Christianity do, today. God existed in their lives, directing their conduct, even when unaware God would have been in their lives. Their judgment will also be based on their response to the gospel presented to them during that time.

Second Category: Pseudo-Christians

This group consists of individuals who identified as Christians but were not part of the first resurrection. They may have been sincere in their faith but were deceived by false teachings or traditions. Like the pseudo-Christians caught alive at Christ's second coming, they will experience profound disappointment, discovering having been excluded from the first resurrection.

Jesus warned, *"Not everyone who says to me, 'Lord, Lord,' will enter the kingdom of heaven, but only the one who does the will of my Father who is in heaven"* (Matthew 7:21, NIV). These individuals will face a harsh reality, but some may still find redemption through humility and repentance. This is why Christianity should never be taken as a casual matter.

Third Category: Those Who Rejected God's Spirit

This group includes individuals who consciously rejected God's Spirit and lived in deliberate rebellion against Him. These individuals are basically those identified as Christians, but having deliberately spurned the truth, possibly out of pride. They will be resurrected to face eternal punishment, having spurned God's grace during their lifetimes.

Jesus said, *"Anyone who speaks a word against the Son of Man will be forgiven, but anyone who speaks against the Holy Spirit will not be forgiven, either in this age or in the age to come"* (Matthew 12:32, NIV).

Hebrews 10:26-27 reiterates the similar sentiment that Christians should not take lightly. These individuals, having hardened their hearts, will face eternal destruction in the lake of fire (Revelation 20:15).

It is indeed surprising that individuals who have received God's grace and the Holy Spirit choose to pursue rebellion. The nature of humanity can be extremely unpredictable. Similarly, it is incomprehensible how some individuals become influenced by Satan to rebel after the millennial reign of Jesus Christ.

The Nature of Judgment

The Great White Throne Judgment is not a trick to condemn people unfairly. It is a time of truth and revelation, where the books are opened, and every individual's life is examined (Revelation 20:12).

Those who accept God's grace will find eternal life, while those who reject it will face eternal separation from Him. It can, indeed, be frustrating to see our loved ones choosing the path of condemnation, rather than God's grace.

The parable of Lazarus and the rich man (Luke 16:19-31) illustrates the stark contrast between those who embrace God's Kingdom and those who cling to worldly values.

The rich man, who lived in luxury, found himself in torment after death, while Lazarus, who suffered in poverty, was comforted in Abraham's bosom. This parable underscores the importance of humility and the dangers of self-centeredness..

The contrasting attitudes of the two thieves facing judgment with Christ reveal the profundity of the grace offered by Christ (Luke 23:39-44), Both thieves had been pronounced as deserving to die, but one of the two was promised salvation, based only on his attitude towards Jesus.

The Final Destiny

After the judgment, the old order of things will pass away, and a new heaven and earth will be established (Revelation 21:1). The redeemed will inherit eternal life, free from the limitations of physical existence. Those who reject God's grace will be consumed in the lake of fire, a fate reserved for the devil, the beast, and the false prophet (Revelation 20:10).

Paul reminds us,
"There are also heavenly bodies and there are earthly bodies, but the splendour of the heavenly bodies is one kind, and the splendour of the earthly bodies is another" (1 Corinthians 15:40, NIV).

To love this world, is another way of choosing to be condemned with it. However, to be condemned by this world, ensures salvation. The new creation will be a spiritual reality, far surpassing the temporary and materialistic world we know today.

The Call to Humility and Faith

The resurrection and judgment reveal the ultimate triumph of God's justice and mercy. They call us to live lives of humility, as not to be too comfortable in the flesh. This requires faith, and obedience, trusting in Christ's sacrifice for our salvation. As Jesus said, *"I am the way, the truth, and the life. No one comes to the Father except through me"* (John 14:6, NIV).

In a world frequently driven by pride and self-centeredness, the gospel message calls us to embrace God's Kingdom—a Kingdom founded on love, humility, and eternal truth. This Kingdom remains inaccessible to those who are self-centred and who categorize others based on class and status.

CHAPTER 11

THE SEVEN-DAY WEEK AND THE SABBATH

The observance of the Seventh-Day Sabbath is a topic that goes beyond mere acknowledgement or rejection. It raises questions about obedience to God's commandments and the motives of those who keep the Sabbath. The law, including the Sabbath, was designed for physical humans, not spiritual beings. Jesus Himself did not abolish the law but fulfilled it, highlighting its lasting significance.

"I tell you the truth, until heaven and earth disappear, not the smallest letter, not the least stroke of a pen, will by any means disappear from the Law until everything is accomplished" (Matthew 5:18 NIV).

This passage underscores the importance of God's commandments, including the Sabbath. Yet, the Sabbath's significance extends far beyond a day of rest—it is a profound symbol of God's plan for humanity. Like most Scriptural references, the Sabbath carries some Spiritual significance, being the ultimate goal of humanity.

The Sabbath in Creation and Redemption

The seven-day creation narrative, culminating in the Sabbath, is not merely a scientific account but a parabolic revelation of God's work with humanity. The physical world, though marvelous, pales in comparison to the spiritual masterpiece of human creation.

Humanity, made in God's image, is fundamentally spiritual, even as we navigate a material world governed by force and competition. In contrast, God's Kingdom operates on principles of humility and service, rather than being motivated by competition. Jesus taught that true greatness comes through serving others, a concept foreign to a world driven by power and self-interest.

The Sabbath rest, following six days of labour, symbolizes more than physical repose. It points to a deeper spiritual truth: God's ultimate plan for humanity's redemption and rest. This pattern is echoed in the Book of Revelation, where Jesus promises authority to those who overcome:

"He will rule them with an iron sceptre; he will dash them to pieces like pottery" (Revelation 2:27 NIV).

This authority, however, is not an end in itself but a precursor to the establishment of God's eternal Kingdom.

The Millennial Week: A Prophetic Framework

The seven-day week also serves as a prophetic framework for understanding God's timeline for humanity. As Peter writes, *"With the Lord, a day is like a thousand years, and a thousand years are like a day"* (2 Peter 3:8 NIV).

This suggests that the seven-day creation week mirrors a seven-thousand-year divine plan for humanity. While this interpretation is not a scientific claim, it offers a symbolic lens through which to view biblical history.

The First Millennium: From Adam to Noah

This era, defined by the fall of humanity and the flood, signifies humanity's initial struggle with sin. Throughout the ages, human history has been characterized by the persistent provocation of God. Nevertheless, in the first millennium, figures such as Abel, Seth, and Enoch emerged as paragons of faithfulness in a fallen world.

The Second Millennium: From Noah to Babel

After the flood, humanity sought to build a name for itself at Babel. God's intervention—confusing their language—halted their prideful ambitions and scattered them across the earth (Genesis 11:1-9).

The Third Millennium: From Abraham to Jesus

God's covenant with Abraham set the stage for the nation of Israel and the eventual coming of Christ. This period, spanning roughly two thousand years, culminated in the birth, death, and resurrection of Jesus.

The Fourth Millennium: Jesus' Death, Leading towards His Resurrection after the Third Day

Jesus' crucifixion and His resurrection marked the midpoint of the millennial week. His three days in the grave symbolize a three-thousand-year period of waiting before the final resurrection and judgment of the entire humanity.

The Fifth Millennium: The Dark Ages

This era, characterized by spiritual decline and societal upheaval, represents humanity's struggle to live in the light of Christ's resurrection. The early disciples were martyred, so that Christianity could not be accurately heard, until the mid of the second century.

The Sixth Millennium: The Christian Dispensation

We are currently in the final stages of this era, a time of preparation for the return of Christ and the establishment of His millennial reign. Jesus Himself declared that no one could precisely predict His second coming, but the Scriptures reveal our position in prophecy.

The Seventh Millennium: The Millennial Sabbath

The second coming of Jesus points at Him coming to take over the authorities of the governments of the world. This final thousand-year period will be a time of rest and restoration, culminating in the final judgment and the creation of a new heaven and a new earth (Revelation 21:1).

The Sabbath as a Shadow of Things to Come

The Sabbath is not merely a day of rest but a foreshadowing of the ultimate rest humanity will experience in God's Kingdom, under Christ. Just as God rested on the seventh day after six days of creation, humanity will also experience rest after the six millennial days of trials in this world.

This rest is not passive but active—a state of perfect harmony with God and one another, under the perfect leadership of Jesus Christ. Jesus' resurrection on the first day of the week further underscores the Sabbath's significance.

His victory over death inaugurated a new creation, pointing forward to the final restoration of all things. As Paul writes, *"If anyone is in Christ, the new creation has come: The old has gone, the new is here!"* (2 Corinthians 5:17 NIV).

The Sabbath and Christian Unity

While debates over Sabbath observance have often divided Christians, the deeper truth is that the Sabbath points to a shared hope: the restoration of all things in Christ.

Whether one observes the Sabbath or not, the principle of rest and renewal remains central to the Christian faith. As Jesus said, *"The Sabbath was made for man, not man for the Sabbath"* (Mark 2:27 NIV).

Rather than focusing on divisive debates, Christians should seek to understand the Sabbath's symbolic significance and its fulfillment in Christ. The Sabbath reminds us that our ultimate rest is found not in our works but in God's grace.

Conclusion: The Sabbath and the Hope of Eternity

The seven-day week and the Sabbath are more than historical or cultural artefacts—they are divine signposts pointing to God's redemptive plan. From creation to consummation, the Sabbath reminds us of God's faithfulness and the rest that awaits His people.

As we await the return of Christ and the establishment of His Kingdom, let us live in the light of this hope, serving others and resting in the assurance of God's promises.

"There remains, then, a Sabbath rest for the people of God; for anyone who enters God's rest also rests from their works, just as God did from his" (Hebrews 4:9-10 NIV).

CHAPTER 12

MIRACLES AND PARABLES

P eople naturally desire survival, yet they often struggle to achieve it without facing significant challenges. For example, Simon and Andrew were fishermen by trade. When Jesus called them to follow Him, He promised to make them "fishers of men" (Matthew 4:19).

To understand why they abandoned their livelihood to follow Christ, we must first consider the methods of fishing and how they parallel the work of spreading the gospel. Fishing typically involves using bait to attract fish. A skilled fisherman knows that without bait, there is little hope of catching anything. Similarly, miracles served as "bait" to draw people's attention to Jesus and His message.

The miraculous catch of fish in Luke 5:4-11, for instance, convinced Peter and Andrew that Jesus was no ordinary man. After a night of fruitless labour, Jesus instructed them to cast their nets again, resulting in an overwhelming catch. This miracle demonstrated His divine authority and led the brothers to leave their nets and follow Him.

While miracles attracted crowds and demonstrated Jesus' power, they were not the ultimate goal of His mission. Many who witnessed or benefited from His miracles—such as the healing of the sick, the lame, and the blind—experienced temporary joy but failed to grasp the deeper spiritual truths He taught. Miracles were a means to an end, not the end itself.

Jesus warned that even false prophets could perform signs and wonders to deceive people (Matthew 24:24-25). True faith, therefore, is not rooted in fascination with miracles but in a transformed heart and a commitment to follow Christ. As He said, *"Whoever wants to be my disciple must deny themselves and take up their cross and follow me"* (Matthew 16:24, NIV).

The Purpose of Miracles

Miracles served as a powerful tool to validate Jesus' identity and mission. They drew people to Him, much like bait draws fish to a net. However, Jesus' ultimate goal was not to amaze crowds but to lead them to the Kingdom of God.

In the Sermon on the Mount (Matthew 5-7), He delivered profound teachings without performing a single miracle, emphasizing that spiritual transformation is more important than physical signs. The parable of the Wise and Foolish Builders (Matthew 7:24-27) illustrates this principle.

Those who hear Jesus' words and put them into practice are like the wise man who built his house on a solid foundation. In contrast, those who are merely fascinated by miracles but fail to act on His teachings are like the foolish man whose house collapses in the storm.

The Parable of the Sower

The parable of the Sower (Matthew 13:3-9) further explains the significance of God's Kingdom, compared to worldly attractions. The seed represents the Word of God, and the soil represents the condition of the human heart.

Some seeds fall on rocky ground, where they sprout quickly but wither due to lack of roots. Others fall among thorns, where they are choked by the cares of the world. Only the seeds that fall on good soil produce a fruitful harvest.

This parable highlights the importance of having a heart receptive to God's Word. True conversion involves more than emotional responses to miracles; it requires a deep, lasting transformation that bears fruit in one's life.

The Role of Parables

Jesus frequently taught in parables, utilizing simple narratives to impart profound spiritual truths. He was mindful of humanity's carnality and thus did not disclose the secrets of the Kingdom to those unprepared for such deep insights.

It was essential for anyone seeking to follow Him to demonstrate their commitment by forsaking everything, akin to His disciples. When His disciples inquired why He spoke in parables, He responded:

"To you, it has been given to know the secrets of the kingdom of God, but for others, they are in parables so that 'seeing they may not see, and hearing they may not understand'" (Luke 8:10, ESV).

Parables revealed truth to those with open hearts while concealing it from those who were prideful or self-centred. The proud, like the religious leaders of Jesus' day, were quick to judge and criticize but slow to understand and repent. In contrast, the humble were willing to listen, learn, and apply His teachings.

The Danger of Self-Centeredness

Self-centeredness is a significant barrier to understanding God's Kingdom. Those who focus on their own interests and judge others harshly often miss the deeper truths of the gospel. Jesus' interactions with the Pharisees illustrate this point.

Despite witnessing His miracles, they accused Him of working by the power of Beelzebub (Matthew 12:24). Their pride blinded them to the truth and hardened their hearts against Him.

In contrast, Jesus demonstrated compassion and advocacy for sinners. When the religious leaders brought a woman caught in adultery to Him, they demanded her execution according to the law (John 8:4-11).

Instead of condemning her, Jesus challenged them: *"Let any one of you who is without sin be the first to throw a stone at her"* (John 8:7, NIV). His response revealed the hypocrisy of self-righteous judgment and the grace of God's forgiveness.

The Call to Altruism

True Christianity is not about self-preservation or maintaining a pristine reputation. It is about selflessly serving others, even deemed unworthy, by society. Jesus modelled this by associating with tax collectors, sinners, and outcasts. He called His followers to emulate Him, also saying, *"Love your enemies and pray for those who persecute you"* (Matthew 5:44, NIV).

The parable of the Good Samaritan (Luke 10:25-37) underscores this principle. While religious leaders passed by a wounded man, it took a Samaritan—despised by the Jews—to stop to help. His actions demonstrated the kind of love and compassion that defines God's Kingdom.

The Ultimate Miracle

The greatest miracle of all is the transformation of a human heart. While physical healings and miraculous signs point to Jesus' power, the true miracle is the redemption of a soul. Through His death and resurrection, Jesus offers eternal life to all who believe in Him.

As followers of Christ, we are called to be agents of this miracle—sharing His love, advocating for the marginalized and living lives that reflect His grace. In doing so, we participate in the work of the Kingdom, bringing light to a world in need of hope. A true Christian does not draw his or her comfort in miraculous performances, but in doing God's work.

CHAPTER 13

PERSONAL SALVATION VS. GOD'S KINGDOM

Many Christians struggle to distinguish between the gospel of personal salvation and the gospel of God's Kingdom. While personal salvation focuses on individual deliverance, God's Kingdom emphasizes a collective, transformative vision for humanity. The problem with prioritizing personal salvation is that it often fosters self-centeredness, limiting one's perspective to individual survival rather than the well-being of others.

When we focus solely on our own salvation, we fail to recognize that our survival is interconnected with the survival of others. For example, starvation in a community affects everyone, even those who have stockpiled resources for themselves.

The self-sufficient may find their provisions depleted when faced with the desperation of the starving masses. Similarly, the Israelites' failure to sustain their blessings in Canaan was due to their inability to resist the negative influences of surrounding nations. Their story serves as a cautionary tale about the limitations of self-centeredness.

The Limitations of Personal Salvation

The Old Covenant, exemplified by Malachi's call to tithe (Malachi 3:10-12), promised blessings to the Israelites if they obeyed God's laws. However, these blessings were limited to the Israelites and did not extend to neighbouring nations. This self-centred approach ultimately led to their downfall, as they were unable to maintain their covenant with God in the face of external pressures.

Today, many preachers use Malachi's promises to encourage tithing, often for fundraising purposes. While tithing can bring material blessings, it is not the essence of the New Covenant.

Jesus ushered in a new era, declaring, *"The law and the prophets were until John: since that time the kingdom of God is preached, and every man presseth into it"* (Luke 16:16, KJV). The New Covenant transcends personal salvation, calling us to embrace a Kingdom mindset that prioritizes the well-being of all.

The Essence of God's Kingdom

God's Kingdom is not about individual prosperity but about collective transformation. It calls us to take responsibility for the world around us, just as Jesus did when He sacrificed Himself for the sins of humanity. A Kingdom-focused Christian is less concerned with personal gain and more committed to alleviating the suffering of others.

Jesus modelled this selfless love throughout His ministry. He associated with sinners, healed the sick, and even forgave those who crucified Him. His actions demonstrated that God's Kingdom is built on love, compassion, and service to others.

As He taught, *"Love your enemies and pray for those who persecute you, that you may be sons of your Father in heaven"* (Matthew 5:44, NIV). The business of Christianity is not to condemn sinners, but to live a life that influences such sinners to appreciate the value of the gospel.

The Danger of Self-Centeredness

Self-centeredness is a significant barrier to understanding and living out the principles of God's Kingdom. When we focus on personal salvation, we risk becoming prideful and judgmental, like the Pharisees who condemned Jesus for associating with sinners. This mindset not only alienates us from others but also blinds us to the deeper truths of the gospel.

Paul warned against such behaviour, urging Christians to avoid jealousy and division. He wrote, *"I gave you milk, not*

solid food, for you were not yet ready for it... You are still world-
ly. For since there is jealousy and quarrelling among you, are
you not worldly? Are you not acting like mere men?" (1 Corinthians 3:2-4, NIV). True maturity in Christ involves moving
beyond personal salvation to embrace the broader mission of
the gospel.

The Call to Altruism

God's Kingdom is characterized by altruism—selfless
concern for the welfare of others. This stands in stark contrast
to the self-centeredness that often dominates human behaviour. A Kingdom-focused Christian seeks to add value to the
lives of others, even at personal cost.

Jesus exemplified this principle when He healed the
ear of a soldier who had come to arrest Him (Luke 22:49-51).
Despite facing betrayal and suffering, He extended love and
compassion to His enemies. This radical love is the hallmark of
God's Kingdom, challenging us to transcend our natural incli-
nations and reflect God's nature in our interactions with others.

The Priority of God's Kingdom

Jesus taught His followers to prioritize God's Kingdom
above all else: *"Seek first the kingdom of God and His righteous-*
ness, and all these things will be added to you" (Matthew 6:33,
NIV). This means placing the needs of others above our own
and working to create a world where justice, love, and peace
prevail.

The gospel of God's Kingdom is not about personal
blessings but about collective transformation. It calls us to be
agents of change, bringing light to a world in need of hope. As
Paul wrote, *"I have become all things to all people so that by all*
possible means I might save some" (1 Corinthians 9:22, NIV).
This mindset reflects the selfless love that defines God's Kingdom.

The Challenge for Modern Christians

Today, many Christians are caught up in denominationalism and personal salvation, often at the expense of the broader mission of God's Kingdom. They focus on individual blessings and doctrinal differences, neglecting the call to love and serve others unconditionally.

True Christianity transcends denominational boundaries and personal agendas. It is about embodying the love of Christ in a way that transforms lives and communities. As Peter wrote, *"Above all, love each other deeply, because love covers over a multitude of sins"* (1 Peter 4:8, NIV). Loving sinners is the primary aim of Christianity, just as Christ loved us when we were still sinners.

The gospel of personal salvation is a starting point, but it is not the end goal. God's Kingdom calls us to move beyond self-centeredness and embrace a vision of collective transformation. It challenges us to love our enemies, serve the marginalized, and work for the well-being of all.

As followers of Christ, we are called to reflect His selfless love in every aspect of our lives. By prioritizing God's Kingdom, we participate in the fulfilment of His redemptive plan, bringing hope and healing to a broken world.

CHAPTER 14

FORGET ABOUT MINERAL RESOURCES

Countries rich in mineral resources often find themselves caught in severe armed conflicts, with little hope for resolution. For example, the Democratic Republic of the Congo (DRC), a nation abundant in resources like cobalt, diamonds, and gold, has never experienced lasting peace since gaining independence. This situation is perplexing and raises important questions about the true significance of humanity.

A critical question to consider is whether these minerals hold any real value. What good are these resources if the people of the country can only dream of peace? A nation's worth should be measured by the quality of life of its citizens. The greatest misconception in this world is assuming that mineral resources are more valuable than human lives.

There is a harsh truth: an uneducated person holds little value in society. Autocratic rulers exploit their power to extract natural resources at the expense of their citizens, viewing them as lacking worth.

Ironically, these dictators provide substandard education while encouraging people to idolize their leaders. This contributes to keeping the population in poverty. An educated person, though valuable, poses a threat to the authority of these rulers. As a result, these leaders adopt a philosophy of maintaining an uneducated, impoverished populace while indoctrinating them against independent thought.

An autocratic ruler, who exploits the uneducated populace, is often uneducated themselves. Knowledge is truly valuable only when it benefits others, highlighting the importance of education in defining a civilized society.

An autocratic leader might appear civilized to an uninformed population, but they are in dire need of education. This exemplifies the complex challenges our world faces today. Conventional education does not seem to provide good quality education that uplifts the value of an individual.

The Mystery of Jesus' Identity as God's Son

The intrinsic value of humanity is represented through Jesus, who came for that specific purpose. Unfortunately, He remains a mystery to many people. Some view Jesus as an individual worthy of worship, which can sometimes lead to idolatry—where the focus is solely on Jesus as a figure to be revered. It is essential to explore the purpose of Jesus while remembering that He embodies what was created in God's image.

Scientific discoveries are plentiful, contributing to the exciting advancements in information technology. However, our understanding of humanity's existence seems largely undiscovered.

There is far more that we do not know about human existence than we can currently comprehend. How can we invest in research that enhances our understanding of human capabilities? While most cultures invest significantly in education and human development, none fully grasp the true significance of humanity itself.

"What is mankind that you are mindful of them, human beings that you care for them? You have made them a little lower than the angels and crowned them with glory and honour. You made them rulers over the works of your hands; you put everything under their feet" (Psalms 8:4-6, NKJV).

The Creator of all things places humans above everything, including angels. Jesus came to provide light, as the notion of valuing mineral resources above all else reflects the confusion present in the world today. As the light of the world, Jesus offers guidance that, when followed correctly, helps to solve all problems. The most important revelation is to prioritize humanity over material wealth.

Jesus: The Son of Man and the Son of God

Jesus came as both the Son of Man and the Son of God to reveal our human condition. By understanding that we are sons of men, we also recognize that we are sons of God, as demonstrated through the personality of Jesus.

The true purpose of Jesus, described as the way, the truth, and the life, is to represent the ideal person created in God's image. His only reason for appearing was to guide us toward our Father.

The teachings of Jesus provide valuable solutions for humanity, but only those who take Him seriously can truly benefit. His actions leading up to His crucifixion illustrate the path that His followers must embrace.

The physical existence often conflicts with spiritual life, much like night contrasts with day. Jesus' willingness to confront the cross serves as a testament that the road to salvation does not lie in seeking comfort in this world.

The Significance of Human Existence

One of the most significant questions about human existence remains largely unexplored, despite the belief that humans were created to solve problems. Investigating our origins can be challenging, but it should be a top priority. No problem can be effectively addressed without first uncovering the mysteries of humanity. Understanding human nature is crucial for success in any endeavour.

The landmark description of humanity is found in Genesis 1:26-27. Humans were created in God's image, making it wrong to treat another human without acknowledging this principle. This principle does not consider the state of degradation the person concerned might be in.

As long as they are identified as a human and not an animal, they deserve the consideration of divinity. The focus should be on how one can assist a degraded person, rather than condemning them. All answers to human problems are found in this principle alone.

Humanity over Material Wealth

While mineral resources are considered a means to address various issues, it is ultimately humans who bear the responsibility for finding solutions. The challenges faced by humanity appear overwhelming, primarily due to a lack of understanding of human nature.

Humans are designed to confront the world's problems, but to do so effectively; we must first explore the true significance of our existence. In many ways, humans seem peculiar, as though they do not quite belong in this world. This is just as Jesus was clear in declaring not being of this world.

Jesus exemplified the principle of valuing humanity above all else. This was intended to help humanity realize that it is the only principle that leads to life. The accumulation of wealth is popular, yet it is contrary to the principle of placing humanity above it. This explains why Jesus clearly elaborated the distinction between God and mammon (Matthew 6:19-24).

While Satan symbolizes the opponent of God, the principle lies in cherishing material things, which are attractive to physical nature, more than godliness.

The Value of Problem-Solvers

It is often overlooked that those who can solve other people's problems are more valuable than the world's mineral resources. A person's worth is determined by their ability to address others' issues.

The pertinent question is what should be done with individuals who do not meet these expectations. The answer lies with the person posing the question. When encountering someone in a deplorable state, the question should be what can be done to help that person, rather than seeking ways to distance oneself from them.

People are divided by many things, ranging from gender, physical appearance, class, intellectual capabilities, or ignorance. However, all such things are not the reason that suggests dissociation.

The axiomatic principle is found in that darkness disappears in the presence of light, not the other way around.

Jesus became the only personality who projected the light among millions of people existing in darkness. However, if those believing in Him were to practice everything He taught, with precision, the entire world would be illuminated.

Conclusion: The True Measure of Value

The prevailing darkness among humanity attests that what is presented as manifesting Christianity is not authentic. A serious individual decides to discard everything and follow only the teachings of Jesus in the four gospels.

Applying verbatim what Jesus said in those texts can be described as the most difficult task ever undertaken by any human. It requires those willing to discard anything, including their physical existence, to reach the required standard. In other words, any person is as valuable as being willing to sacrifice everything for those around them. This describes the significance of believing in Jesus.

The golden invitation is to shift one's values to doing the opposite of what the physical body demands. This implies disregarding everything considered valuable in this world. A person may die without having produced anything deemed valuable. However, they would have attained true value.

Each individual carries eternal value upon dying after transforming their attitude. There is no need to worry about the opinions of others. Jesus, whose body was placed on the cross, was considered valueless, yet there has never been a person as valuable as Jesus in this world.

CHAPTER 15

THE DELUSIONS OF INTROVERSION

I n my approximately seven decades of life, I have observed that many of humanity's failures stem from introversion— the tendency to focus on one's own interests, thoughts, and feelings. Introversion, often mistaken for mere shyness or quietness, is a deeper issue of self-centeredness that manifests in various harmful ways.

From corruption to social isolation, the consequences of introversion are far-reaching and often overlooked. This chapter explores the dangers of introversion, contrasts it with the benefits of extroversion, and highlights how embracing an outward-focused mindset can lead to personal and societal transformation.

The Problem with Introversion

Introversion is not just a personality trait; it is a mindset that prioritizes self over others. It is the root of many societal ills, including corruption, envy, and hypocrisy. When individuals focus solely on their own needs and desires, they neglect the well-being of others, leading to inequality, exploitation, and conflict.

For example, corruption—a global scourge—is fundamentally a product of introversion. Corrupt individuals amass wealth and power for personal comfort, disregarding the harm they cause to society. As Jesus warned in the parable of the rich fool:

"But God said to him, 'You fool! This very night your life will be demanded from you. Then who will get what you have prepared for yourself?' This is how it will be with whoever stores up things for themselves but is not rich toward God" (Luke 12:20-21, NIV).

This parable illustrates the futility of a self-centred life. The rich man's introversion led him to hoard resources, ignoring his responsibility to use his abundance for the greater good. His story is a cautionary tale for all who prioritize personal gain over communal well-being. Another example is the rise of individualism in modern societies.

In many Western countries, the pursuit of personal success has led to a decline in community engagement and social cohesion. People are increasingly isolated, focusing on their careers and personal goals while neglecting their roles as active, contributing members of society. This introversion has resulted in widespread loneliness, mental health issues, and a lack of trust in institutions.

The Power of Extroversion

In contrast to introversion, extroversion is characterized by an outward focus—a desire to connect with others, share resources, and contribute to the common good. Extroverts thrive on collaboration and communication, making them natural leaders, innovators, and problem-solvers.

Consider the example of successful athletes, musicians, and entrepreneurs. Their achievements are not solely the result of talent or hard work but also their ability to engage with others.

A footballer, for instance, succeeds not just through individual skill but by working as part of a team. Similarly, a musician's artistry is amplified when shared with an audience. These examples demonstrate that success is often a collective effort, rooted in extroversion.

Another powerful example is the global response to natural disasters. When earthquakes, hurricanes, or floods strike, communities often come together to provide aid and support.

This extroverted behaviour—rooted in empathy and solidarity—saves lives and rebuilds societies. It stands in stark contrast to the introverted mindset that prioritizes self-preservation over collective action.

The Dangers of Introversion in Society

Introversion is not just a personal failing; it has societal implications. In Zimbabwe, for instance, the adoption of introverted behaviours—such as exclusivity and elitism—has contributed to social fragmentation and economic decline.

After gaining independence in 1980, many Zimbabweans embraced the introverted lifestyles of the colonial elite, prioritizing personal advancement.

This advancement over communal development shift eroded traditional values of **ubuntu** (communality) and led to widespread inequality and disillusionment. The rise of denominationalism in Christianity is another example of introversion's harmful effects.

Many churches focus inward, prioritizing doctrinal purity and institutional growth over the needs of the broader community. This introversion undermines the church's mission to be a light to the world, as Jesus commanded:

"You are the light of the world. A town built on a hill cannot be hidden. Neither do people light a lamp and put it under a bowl. Instead, they put it on its stand, and it gives light to everyone in the house" (Matthew 5:14-15, NIV).

When Christians retreat into denominational enclaves, they fail to fulfil their calling to serve and transform society.

The Hypocrisy of Introversion

Introversion often leads to hypocrisy, as individuals project a false image of themselves to gain approval or avoid scrutiny. Jesus repeatedly condemned this behaviour, particularly among the religious leaders of His time:

"Woe to you, teachers of the law and Pharisees, you hypocrites! You clean the outside of the cup and dish, but inside they are full of greed and self-indulgence. Blind Pharisee! First clean the inside of the cup and dish, and then the outside also will be clean" (Matthew 23:25-26, NIV).

The Pharisees' introversion made them more concerned with appearances than authenticity. They sought to impress others while neglecting justice, mercy, and faithfulness. This hypocrisy alienated them from God and from the people they were called to serve.

The Call to Extroversion in Christianity

True Christianity is inherently extroverted. It calls believers to look beyond themselves and serve others selflessly. Jesus modelled this outward-focused lifestyle, reaching out to the marginalized, healing the sick, and challenging oppressive systems.

His ministry was marked by compassion, inclusivity, and a commitment to the common good. The apostle Paul echoed this call to extroversion, urging believers to embrace their role as ambassadors of reconciliation:

"All this is from God, who reconciled us to himself through Christ and gave us the ministry of reconciliation: that God was reconciling the world to himself in Christ, not counting people's sins against them. And he has committed to us the message of reconciliation" (2 Corinthians 5:18-19, NIV).

As Christ's ambassadors, Christians are called to bridge divides, heal relationships, and promote justice. This mission requires an extroverted mindset—one that prioritizes the needs of others over personal comfort or gain.

Practical Steps toward Extroversion

Cultivate Empathy: Seek to understand the experiences and perspectives of others. Listen actively and respond with compassion.

Serve Others: Look for opportunities to contribute to your community, whether through volunteering, mentoring, or supporting local initiatives.

Build Relationships: Foster meaningful connections with people from diverse backgrounds. Embrace collaboration and teamwork.

Challenge Injustice: Speak out against systems and practices that harm others. Advocate for fairness and equality.

Live Authentically: Reject hypocrisy and strive to align your actions with your values. Be a person of integrity and transparency.

Conclusion: Embracing an Outward-Focused Life

Introversion, while often seen as harmless or even virtuous, is a delusion that undermines personal growth and societal progress. By contrast, extroversion—rooted in empathy, service, and collaboration—offers a path to fulfilment and transformation.

As individuals and communities, we must reject the self-centeredness of introversion and embrace the outward-focused mindset modelled by Jesus.

In doing so, we can create a world marked by justice, compassion, and shared prosperity. Let us move beyond the delusions of introversion and live as lights in the darkness, shining brightly for all to see.

CHAPTER 16

POVERTY AND WEALTH

Poverty remains a persistent reality in our world, even in societies advanced in technology. Why do some people thrive in wealth while others languish in poverty? The answer lies in how we define wealth. From a worldly perspective, wealth is often measured by the accumulation of money, property, and possessions.

However, from a biblical perspective, true wealth is defined by one's ability to address the needs of others and contribute to the well-being of society. The principles of the New Civilization, rooted in altruism, offer a transformative approach to understanding and addressing poverty and wealth.

While these principles may seem idealistic, they are practical and applicable in our daily lives. Wealth, in this context, is not about hoarding resources but about using them to create value for others.

The World's Definition of Wealth

The dictionary defines wealth as the accumulation of money, property, and valuable possessions. However, this definition often leads to a self-centred mindset, where individuals focus on personal gain rather than collective well-being. Consider the following scenario:

Three men wish to travel from Harare to Bulawayo but fail due to a lack of funds. The first cannot afford $20 for public transport, the second cannot raise $60 for fuel, and the third cannot secure $200 for a plane ticket.

The three are equally poor, as they could not afford to raise the required amount to travel to Bulawayo. Yet, their inability to travel highlights a deeper issue: the limitations of a self-centred approach to wealth. Their needs are assessed based on their status, yet they are ultimately reduced to common physical limitations.

God's Definition of Wealth

Jesus redefined wealth when He praised a poor widow for having given more—all she had—to the temple treasury (Luke 21:1-4). In the eyes of the world, she was poor, but in God's eyes, she was rich because of her generosity and selflessness. True wealth, according to Jesus, is measured by one's capacity to give, not by what one accumulates.

The New Civilization teaches that wealth is not about material possessions but about the ability to solve problems and add value to the lives of others. A wealthy person, in this sense, is one who uses their resources, talents, and abilities to benefit others. This principle is evident in successful businesses that prioritize customer satisfaction and ethical practices.

The Law of Giving and Receiving

Wealth is generated through the exchange of value. The more one gives the wealthier he or she becomes. When we give, we sow seeds that eventually bear fruit. Conversely, when we focus solely on receiving without giving, we consume resources without creating lasting value. This principle is universal and applies to individuals, businesses, and nations.

For example, a business that prioritizes customer needs and delivers quality products or services will thrive. In contrast, a business that cuts corners or exploits customers will eventually fail. The same principle applies to individuals: those who focus on solving problems and serving others will attract respect, opportunities, and financial rewards.

The Danger of Self-Centeredness

Self-centeredness is a root cause of poverty. When individuals or societies focus solely on personal gain, they create systems that perpetuate inequality and suffering. Philanthropy, while well-intentioned, can sometimes reinforce dependency rather than empowerment. True wealth is not about giving handouts but about creating opportunities for others to thrive.

Inherited wealth, for instance, can lead to impoverishment if the next generation does not understand the principles that created it. As Jesus warned, *"Watch out! Be on your guard against all kinds of greed; life does not consist in an abundance of possessions"* (Luke 12:15, NIV). Wealth without wisdom and responsibility is fleeting and often destructive.

The Role of Talent and Professionalism

True wealth is built on talent, passion, and professionalism. Every individual is uniquely gifted, and these gifts are meant to be used for the benefit of others. Whether one is a cleaner, an artist, or a CEO, it is professionalism and a commitment to excellences that set such individuals apart and create lasting value.

For example, a skilled sewage cleaner who approaches their work with passion and professionalism can transform a necessary but often overlooked service into a lucrative and respected career. Similarly, a talented athlete or artist can achieve wealth and influence by using their gifts to inspire and entertain others.

The Illusion of Quick Wealth

Many people fall into poverty by chasing quick wealth through gambling, unethical business practices, or illegal activities. While these paths may offer temporary gains, they ultimately lead to ruin. True wealth is built on integrity, hard work, and a commitment to adding value to the lives of others.

The parable of the dishonest manager (Luke 16:1-9) illustrates this principle. While the manager's actions were unethical, his shrewdness in using resources to build relationships earned him commendation. The lesson is clear: wealth is not about exploiting others but about creating value that benefit others and building meaningful connections.

The Scale of Poverty and Wealth

Wealth and poverty can be understood as points on a scale. At one end is poverty, characterized by a focus on receiving and dependency. At the other end is wealth, characterized by a focus on giving and creating value.

The more one gives the more disposed to wealth he or she becomes. The more one receives, the more disposed to poverty one becomes. The stagnation is found in the midpoint representing self-sufficiency, where one neither gives nor receives.

To move from poverty to wealth, individuals must shift their mindset from self-centeredness to altruism. This involves identifying their unique talents, using them to solve problems, and contributing to the well-being of others. This is what makes life meaningful.

The Role of Leadership and Responsibility

Poverty is often perpetuated by poor leadership and a lack of responsibility. In many African nations, for example, abundant natural resources coexist with widespread poverty due to corruption, self-centeredness, and a failure to invest in people.

True leaders are those who use their leadership skills and resources to address the needs of their communities. They understand that wealth is not about personal gain but about creating opportunities for others to thrive.

As Hosea warned, *"My people are destroyed from lack of knowledge"* (Hosea 4:6, NIV). Ignorance and self-centeredness are the root causes of poverty, while knowledge and altruism are the pathways to wealth.

Wealth in the New Civilization

In the New Civilization, wealth is redefined as the ability to love, serve and create value for others. Wealth is not measured by material possessions but by the impact one has on the lives of others. True Christians, guided by the Holy Spirit, are called to transcend the limitations of a self-centred world and embody the principles of God's Kingdom.

As Paul wrote, *"It is more blessed to give than to receive"* (Acts 20:35, NIV). Normal humans find life satisfying, only when adding value to their fellow men. This principle lies at the heart of the New Civilization, offering a transformative vision of wealth that benefits all of humanity.

CHAPTER 17

HAPPINESS COMES FROM MAKING OTHERS HAPPY

W e live in a world governed by laws that, when followed, can make life deeply fulfilling. Among these, the most fundamental principle for humanity is the Golden Rule: *"Treat others as you would like to be treated"* (Matthew 7:12). This timeless wisdom, found in various cultures and religions, underscores the interconnectedness of human happiness. When we bring joy to others, we inevitably find joy ourselves.

Consider the example of a sportsperson. Their happiness is intrinsically tied to the satisfaction of their fans. The better they perform, the more they delight their audience, and the greater their own sense of accomplishment and joy. This principle extends beyond sports—it applies to every field of endeavor.

Whether in art, science, education, or service, the happiness we derive from our work is magnified when it positively impacts others. However, to truly excel and find fulfillment, one must discover and nurture their innate talents. Passion is the driving force behind mastery.

Without it, even the most lucrative or prestigious pursuits can feel hollow. Sadly, many individuals spend their lives in careers that do not align with their natural abilities. They may earn a living, but they often lack genuine happiness.

For instance, a person gifted in cleaning might feel societal pressure to pursue a higher-paying job, even if it brings them no joy. Yet, true happiness is not found in wealth but in the satisfaction of using one's talents to serve others.

The Power of Passion and Purpose

Happiness flourishes when individuals engage in work that aligns with their passions and talents. The specific field matters less than the joy it brings to others. Every profession, no matter how humble, has the potential to make a difference. For example, in Zimbabwe, there are teachers who go above and beyond to educate their students, despite being underpaid by a financially strained government.

Their dedication stems not from monetary reward but from their love for teaching and the impact they have on their students' lives. Over time, their commitment earns them the respect and gratitude of parents, who seek them out for their exceptional service.

This echoes the biblical principle: *"Seek first the Kingdom of God, and all these things shall be added unto you"* (Matthew 6:33). Here, the "Kingdom of God" can be interpreted as living a life of service and treating others with kindness and respect.

The Cost of Ignoring One's Calling

Ignoring one's true calling in pursuit of wealth or status often leads to dissatisfaction. I recall a talented young soccer player in Zimbabwe who abandoned his passion to take a well-paying cleaning job overseas. While he earned a steady income, he lacked fulfillment.

Meanwhile, a friend who persevered in soccer eventually made it to the Premier League, opening doors to international opportunities. The first young man's story serves as a cautionary tale: when we neglect our talents, we risk losing not only our happiness but also the chance to make a meaningful impact on others.

The True Measure of Success

Success is not measured by wealth or status but by the joy we bring to others. Consider the story of Tabitha (also known as Dorcas) from the early Christian church. She was a woman "full of good works and charitable deeds" (Acts 9:36). When she passed away, the community mourned her deeply, and her acts of kindness were so impactful that Peter was moved to pray for her resurrection.

Tabitha's life exemplifies the profound truth that happiness comes from serving others. Her legacy continues to inspire us today, reminding us that the purpose of life lies in making others happy.

The Pitfalls of Greed and Selfishness

In contrast, those who prioritize personal gain over the well-being of others often find themselves trapped in a cycle of unhappiness. Jesus addressed this in the parable of the rich fool (Luke 12:13-21). The man in the story hoarded his wealth, believing it would secure his happiness.

Yet, his life was cut short, and his riches brought him no lasting joy. Jesus' message is clear: *"One's life does not consist in the abundance of possessions"* (Luke 12:15). True happiness comes from generosity and service, not from accumulating wealth.

Similarly, the parable of the unjust steward (Luke 16:1-13) highlights the importance of using resources to build relationships and bring joy to others. Though the steward's actions were morally questionable, his shrewdness in securing the goodwill of others underscores a deeper truth: happiness is found in making others happy.

The Legacy We Leave Behind

The legacy we leave is not measured by the wealth we accumulate but by the lives we touch. A parent's greatest gift to their children is not an inheritance but the wisdom to live a life of service. Teaching children to value others and contribute to their well-being ensures that they lead meaningful and fulfilling lives.

As the Bible reminds us, *"Whatever your hand finds to do, do it with your might"* (Ecclesiastes 9:10). When we pour our energy into serving others, we create a legacy that outlasts material possessions.

Conclusion: The Path to True Happiness

Happiness is not a solitary pursuit; it is a shared experience. By making others happy, we unlock the door to our own joy. Whether through teaching, healing, creating, or serving, every act of kindness ripples outward, touching lives in ways we may never fully comprehend.

As we navigate life, let us remember the words of Jesus: *"It is more blessed to give than to receive"* (Acts 20:35). In giving of ourselves—our time, talents, and compassion—we find the true essence of happiness.

SAFETY PRECAUTIONS

In a world plagued by poverty and desperation, many are willing to engage in risky or even superstitious practices in the hope of finding relief. Some turn to mythological remedies or dubious schemes, driven by the belief that anything is better than their current suffering.

This desperation highlights the profound impact of poverty and the lengths to which people will go to escape it. Christianity, while offering hope and redemption, is not without its own risks.

Contrary to the perception that it is a safe and honourable path, following Christ can be one of the most challenging and perilous journeys one can undertake. Jesus Himself warned that His followers would face persecution, ridicule, and even death (Matthew 10:22).

The Risks of Christianity

Christianity is not a career choice or a means to achieve worldly success. It is a calling that demands complete surrender of personal ambitions, comfort, and even dignity. Jesus made this clear when He said:

"If anyone comes to me and does not hate his father and mother, his wife and children, his brothers and sisters—yes, even his own life—he cannot be my disciple. Whoever does not carry his cross and follow me cannot be my disciple" (Luke 14:26-27, NIV).

This radical call to discipleship stands in stark contrast to the comfortable, self-centred lifestyles many aspire to. Those who enter Christian ministry for personal gain or social status are likely to face disappointment and spiritual peril.

The Deception of Honour

One of the greatest misconceptions about Christianity is that it brings honour and respect in this world. While some church leaders may enjoy prestige and privilege, true Christianity often involves suffering and disgrace. The cross, the central symbol of the faith, represents not glory but shame and sacrifice.

Jesus warned that many are called but few are chosen (Matthew 22:14). This implies that not all who claim to follow Christ will ultimately be accepted by Him. Those who seek honour and recognition in this life may find themselves excluded from the Kingdom of God, although not exhaustive.

The Hazards of Christian Ministry

Entering Christian ministry is not a decision to be taken lightly. It comes with significant risks and responsibilities. Below are some of the hazards that aspiring ministers should consider:

1. **The Danger of Pride:** Success in ministry can lead to pride, which is a deadly trap for God's servants. Jesus cautioned His disciples against rejoicing in their achievements, reminding them to focus on their eternal reward (Luke 10:20).

2. **Loss of Dignity and Honour:** Following Christ often means surrendering personal dignity and facing ridicule or persecution. The apostles, with the exception of John, all died as martyrs for their faith.

3. **Rejection and Ostracism:** Teaching spiritual truths that challenge traditional beliefs can lead to rejection and isolation. Jesus Himself was despised and rejected by many (Matthew 8:20).

4. **High Expectations:** Church leaders are held to a higher standard and are expected to lead by example.

This requires sacrificing personal comfort and interests for the sake of others (Luke 12:48).

5. **The Risk of Stumbling Others:** Leaders who fail to live up to their calling can become stumbling blocks to others, inviting severe consequences (Matthew 18:6).

6. **Relentless Scrutiny:** Church leaders are often subjected to intense scrutiny and unfounded accusations. Maintaining integrity and humility is essential in such a role.

7. **Spiritual Warfare:** Satan actively targets church leaders, seeking to destroy their influence and lead them astray. Vigilance and prayer are crucial for spiritual survival (Revelation 12:13).

8. **Vulnerability to False Accusations:** In a world of injustice, church leaders are particularly vulnerable to false accusations, such as financial misconduct or moral failings.

The True Reward of Ministry

Despite these risks, serving in Christian ministry is a profound privilege. It offers the opportunity to participate in God's redemptive work and to make an eternal impact on the lives of others. However, this reward is not measured in worldly terms but in spiritual fulfilment and the joy of serving Christ.

Paul, who endured immense suffering for the gospel, described his ministry as a "noble task" (1 Timothy 3:1). Yet, his life was marked by hardship, persecution, and ultimately, martyrdom. His example reminds us that true ministry is not about personal gain but about selfless service and sacrifice.

The Call to Discipleship

Christianity is not a path to comfort or prosperity but a call to radical discipleship. It requires surrendering one's life to Christ and embracing the cross, no matter the cost:

"Whoever finds his life will lose it, and whoever loses his life for my sake will find it" (Matthew 10:39, NIV).

Those who enter ministry must do so with a clear understanding of the risks and a willingness to endure hardship for the sake of the gospel. Anyone who accepts baptism in the name of the Father, Son and the Holy Spirit, becomes a minister, in this regard. Christianity is not a decision to be made lightly or for selfish reasons.

The Importance of Focus

In ministry, the focus must always remain on Christ, not on human leaders or personal ambitions. Each is called to face trials that may be different from one's compatriots. Peter learned this lesson when Jesus rebuked him for being concerned about the fate of another disciple:

"If I want him to remain alive until I return, what is that to you? You must follow me" (John 21:22, NIV).

Each Christian is called to follow Christ in their own unique way, without comparing themselves to others. Whether one's path leads to abundance or hardship, the ultimate goal is to glorify God and fulfil His purpose. This is akin to being conscripted into the army.

Christian ministry is a high calling that comes with significant risks and responsibilities. It is not a path to worldly honour or success but a journey of sacrifice, service, and surrender. Those who answer this call must do so with a clear understanding of the challenges that go with it and a steadfast commitment to Christ.

As Jesus said, *"The harvest is plentiful, but the workers are few"* (Matthew 9:37, NIV). Those who are willing to take up the cross and follow Him will find true honour, not in this world but in the Kingdom of God. Christianity has fewer people than most people assume.

CHAPTER 19

SEVEN OBSTACLES OF CHRISTIAN FAITH

The cause of Christianity rests solely on Jesus Christ, who accomplished everything necessary for humanity's salvation. Faith, however, must be rooted in sincerity and understanding. It is not enough to declare allegiance to Christ; one must grasp the reasons for that faith and embrace it with a heart free from superstition or self-reliance.

Many claim to follow Christ yet remain trapped in past sins, mistakenly believing that salvation can be earned through their own efforts. Scripture reminds us:

"For God so loved the world that He gave His only begotten Son, that whoever believes in Him should not perish but have everlasting life. For God did not send His Son into the world to condemn the world, but that the world through Him might be saved" (John 3:16-17, NKJV).

Condemnation, however, remains a reality for most people. Why does this occur when salvation is available to all? The answer lies in a lack of faith.

As heirs of Abraham's promise (Galatians 3:29), Christians have an assurance of deliverance anchored in faith alone, not in their works or merit. This necessitates an exploration of the obstacles hindering access to salvation.

Abraham serves as a profound example of unwavering faith, sustained by a belief in God. Despite his imperfections, he trusted God completely, even when asked to do the unimaginable (Genesis 22:1–19).

His obedience was not based on human logic but on a deep, unshakable belief in God's promises. Like Abraham, we are called to trust God, even when His instructions may appear as defying human understanding.

God speaks clearly to those who listen with sincerity. While His message may seem illogical to others, it is unmistakable to those who seek Him with an open heart. Abraham's faith was not blind hypnosis; it was a deliberate, logical submission to the One who called him.

At conversion, we become Abraham's spiritual descendants, inheriting the same promise of salvation. Yet, like Abraham, we are tested. These trials are not meant to break us but to refine our faith and draw us closer to God's grand plan for humanity:

"Praise be to the God and Father of our Lord Jesus Christ...For He chose us in Him before the creation of the world to be holy and blameless in His sight. In love, He predestined us for adoption to son-ship through Jesus Christ, in accordance with His pleasure and will—to the praise of His glorious grace, which He has freely given us..." (Ephesians 1:3-6, NIV).

Predestination does not mean that God has predetermined some for salvation and others for condemnation. Such a view contradicts the universal offer of salvation in John 3:16-17. Rather, predestination underscores God's sovereign plan to bring humanity into His family through faith. The only obstacle to this deliverance is a lack of faith, often rooted in dishonesty, manifested by a divided loyalty.

God cannot tolerate lukewarm faith (Revelation 3:15-16). This is what caused the Israel's downfall (Hebrews 4:1-2). Like the twelve spies sent to survey Canaan (Numbers 13–14), we are called to trust God's promises.

Ten of the spies returned with a faithless report, focusing on the giants rather than God's power. Their lack of faith infected the entire nation, thereby, delaying their entry into the Promised Land. Only Caleb and Joshua, who trusted God, were allowed to enter into the Promised Land with the next generation.

Predestination is God's invitation to the entire humanity. Failures arise not from God's exclusion but from our lack of faith. Through the cross, God extends His mercy to all, barring only those who deliberately reject His offer (Hebrews 10:26-27).

[Seven Obstacles of Christian Faith]

Throughout history, God has used individuals—both good and bad—to fulfil His purposes. Yet His ultimate plan is to save the entire humanity, even those who pierced Him. Today, Christians face seven significant obstacles that can hinder their journey of faith. These traps are as relevant now as they were in biblical times:

Obstacle #1: An Unforgiving Attitude

The idea of forgiving others is central to Christianity. Jesus taught that we must forgive others to receive God's forgiveness (Matthew 6:12). When Adam and Eve sinned, it was God who sought them out, demonstrating His willingness to restore the broken relationship (Genesis 3:9).

True Christians strive towards forgive others even before they ask for forgiveness. The idea of forgiving others is not about asserting superiority but about releasing others from the burden of sin.

It requires understanding the offender's condition and showing love, even when it is undeserved. After all, every person is created in God's image and deserves respect, regardless of their actions. As 1 John 3:16 reminds us, we are our brothers' keepers.

Obstacle #2: The Desire for Recognition

Some people seek accolades for their Christian service, but Jesus warned against such motives (Matthew 7:21-23). Those who perform great deeds in His name yet crave human praise risk rejection. Their rewards end with earthly applauses (Matthew 6:1-4).

However, even selfish motives can yield miraculous results (Philippians 1:15-18), but this does not guarantee salvation. True faith directs all glory to Christ, not to oneself or to any other personality.

Jesus illustrated this in the parable of the workers in the vineyard (Matthew 20:1-16), showing that God's grace, not human effort, determines our worth.

Obstacle #3: Self-Pity

Self-pity traps believers in a cycle of bitterness and despair. It blinds them to the suffering of others and fosters resentment toward God for perceived injustices. Yet, Jesus modelled compassion towards sinners, rather than Himself, even in His darkest hour (Luke 23:28-31).

The Christian life is not about comfort or self-indulgence. It is about enduring trials with faith and using our experiences to minister to others (Matthew 5:11-12).

Obstacle #4: Degrading Others

The idea of judging others harshly stems from pride, which Jesus projected as to a log in one's eye (Matthew 7:1-5). Moses and Aaron fell into this trap at the waters of Meribah, allowing their frustration with the Israelites to overshadow their trust in God (Numbers 20:9-12).

True love necessitates humility and empathy. We must remember that we, too, are sinners in need of grace. As James 4:11-12 warns us that judging other people is what serves to treacherously place us in positions of being above God's law.

Obstacle #5: Self-Degradation

Self-degradation commonly manifests as fear— portrayed in fear of the unknown, fear of authority, or fear of the majority. It paralyzes believers, preventing them from stepping out in faith.

David's courage against Goliath (1 Samuel 17:26-37) contrasts sharply with Saul's self-doubt or invalidation (1 Samuel 9:21). This comes from not being aware of one's origin God equips those He calls, as they allow God to work in their lives without hindrance.

As Paul declared, *"I can do all things through Christ who strengthens me"* (Philippians 4:13). As Christians, we are called to trust in God's power, not our own.

Obstacle #6: Doubt

Doubt may be the greatest adversary of faith. Peter walked on water until doubt infiltrated his mind (Matthew 14:27-31). Similarly, we often falter when we divert our focus from Jesus, focusing on things that appear more daunting to us.

Doubt arises from divided loyalties and must be conquered through unwavering trust in God's promises. Doubt permits Satan to infiltrate our minds, as it generates fear, which pertains only to the physical nature and often arises when heeding discouragement or dissenting voices.

Obstacle #7: Pride

Pride can be labelled as the root of all other obstacles. It primarily blinds a person to their need for God and fosters a sense of superiority. The Pharisees' rejection of Jesus was rooted in pride, as was the Laodiceans' self-sufficiency (Revelation 3:17).

Humility is the antidote to pride. Only by recognizing our dependence on God can we overcome these obstacles and fully embrace the Christian journey.

By identifying and addressing these seven obstacles, believers can experience the joy and freedom to enjoy in a faith-filled life. The path to God's Kingdom is not for the faint-hearted, but for those who courageously trust in His promises and live in the reality of His grace.

CHAPTER 20

THE SEVEN ATTRIBUTES
OF ABRAHAM

To build a strong foundation of faith, we can look to the life of Abraham, whose story offers profound lessons for believers today. However, it's important to avoid the misconception that Abraham was spiritually superior or morally perfect.

Abraham is our spiritual father not because of his righteousness but because of his submission to God's grace, which leads to our salvation, began with him. Righteousness cannot be attributed to any human virtue; it is a gift from God. Abraham received God's favour through his belief and faith in God.

As Scripture says:
"What does the Scripture say? 'Abraham believed God, and it was credited to him as righteousness'" (Romans 4:3, NIV).
"If you belong to Christ, then you are Abraham's seed and heirs according to the promise" (Galatians 3:29, NIV).

Abraham's life should not be seen as a model for Christian living in every aspect. The primary lesson to be drawn from Abraham is his faith and trust in God's word. His tests and challenges were specific to his historical and cultural context. We are Abraham's spiritual descendants, not because we imitate his lifestyle, but because we share his faith in the one true God, whose ultimate revelation is Jesus Christ.

Some Christian communities justify practices such as polygamy by citing Abraham or his grandson Jacob. However, biblical figures should not be emulated as if they represent ideal humanity. They were ordinary people with flaws and failures, just like us. We identify with Abraham not in his perfection but in his humanity, particularly in his reliance on God's grace.

By faith, Abraham received grace. By the same faith, we too receive grace. God does not show favouritism (Acts 10:34-35; 1 Peter 1:17). Abraham's story reveals how God's grace covers human inadequacies when we exercise faith.

If God's favour remained with Abraham despite his shortcomings, the same is true for us, regardless of our own flaws. As Abraham's seed, we inherit the privileges of his covenant. Below are seven key attributes of Abraham that can guide and inspire our faith journey:

Attribute #1: A Direct Call.

Abraham's journey began with a direct call from God: *"Go from your country, your people, and your father's household to the land I will show you"* (Genesis 12:1, NIV).

Abraham followed God's command to depart from his people without knowing his destination. He trusted God's voice over human reasoning or contrary opinions. This call was not based on Abraham's righteousness or merit but on God's sovereign choice. Similarly, Christians are called by God:

"No one can come to me unless the Father who sent me draws them" (John 6:44, NIV).

This calling is not a reward for virtuous deeds but an invitation to believe and trust in God's truth. Like Abraham, we face uncertainties and challenges as we follow God's call. Living out our faith in a sinful world is impossible without Christ's guidance and strength.

Abraham's promised land, Canaan, did not immediately appear advantageous. Likewise, the heavenly promises we receive as Christians are not always visible to the physical eye. Faith requires us to trust in what we cannot yet see.

Attribute #2: Unconditional Promises.

Upon Abraham's arrival in Canaan, he found no immediate signs of prosperity. Instead, he encountered a severe famine (Genesis 12:6-10). This did not lead to contempt against God, but in his weakness, Abraham relied on human reasoning rather than seeking God's counsel. He went to Egypt and even lied about his wife, Sarai, to protect himself.

However, God's unconditional promises remained intact. Abraham's mistakes did not nullify God's covenant. This reminds us that God's grace should be regarded as sufficient even more so, during our times of weakness:

"My grace is sufficient for you, for my power is made perfect in weakness" (2 Corinthians 12:9, NIV).

Like Abraham, we are susceptible to lapses in faith. However, God's faithfulness guarantees that His promises will be fulfilled, despite our shortcomings. The weaker we are, the stronger we become in the presence of God.

Attribute #3: Exposure to Human Reasoning.

God promised Abraham, who had no children, to have descendants who would become as numerous as the stars (Genesis 15:5). Yet, when the promise seemed delayed, Abraham and Sarah turned to human reasoning. They produced Ishmael through Hagar, a decision that led to lasting consequences (Genesis 16:1-6).

Similarly, Christians often rely on human logic rather than waiting on God. After Jesus' ascension, the disciples appointed Matthias to replace Judas, relying on their own reasoning rather than waiting for the Holy Spirit to guide them as Jesus had advised (Acts 1:12-26).

While God can work through our mistakes, His plans are best fulfilled when we trust His timing and guidance. Like Abraham, there are times when we disappoint God, but we are covered by His grace as long as we remain humble.

Attribute #4: Gentleness.

Abraham demonstrated gentleness in resolving conflicts. When disputes arose between his herdsmen and Lot's, Abraham allowed Lot to choose the best land, even though he was entitled to make the first choice, as the leader (Genesis 13:5-11).

This act of humility and generosity reflects the fruit of the Spirit (Galatians 5:22). True Christians prioritize others' interests above their own, following Paul's exhortation:

"Do nothing out of selfish ambition or vain conceit. Rather, in humility value others above yourselves" (Philippians 2:3, NIV).

Attribute #5: Testing.

Abraham's faith was tested when God asked him to sacrifice Isaac, the son of promise (Genesis 22:1-10). This test sought to reveal the depth of Abraham's trust in God.

Abraham did not waiver, as He believed that even if Isaac died, God could raise him from the dead (Hebrews 11:17-19). Human reasoning was uncalled for.

Like Abraham, we are tested in our faith, though not in the same manner as he was. These trials serve to refine our trust in God and prepare us to receive the promises designated to each of us.

Attribute #6: Futuristic Promises.

Abraham did not live to see the full fulfilment of God's promises. Yet, he died in faith, confident that God's word would come to pass (Hebrews 11:13). As Christians, we too live by faith in promises that are yet to be realized.

Our hope is not in what we see but in the certainty of God's faithfulness in His promises. To the faithful ones, the demise of our physical bodies does not remove the trust in God.

Attribute #7: Assurance of the Promise.

God's promises to Abraham were fulfilled in ways he could never have imagined. Today, countless people trace their spiritual heritage to Abraham, fulfilling the promise that his descendants would be as numerous as the stars (Hebrews 11:12).

We have the advantage of seeing how God's plan unfolded through history, culminating in Jesus Christ. This assurance ought to strengthen our faith and remind us that God's promises are unchanging.

A Christian lives without worry, though facing multiple challenges of physical nature. The martyred Christians died without losing the promised hope.

Abraham's life teaches us that faith is not about perfection but about trusting in God's promises. His story reminds us that God's grace covers our weaknesses and that His plans are fulfilled in His timing, regardless of our own shortcomings or abilities.

By following Abraham's example of faith, we can confidently walk in the assurance of God's promises, knowing that He who began a good work in us will carry it to completion (Philippians 1:6).

CHAPTER 21

EARTHLY PARENTS ARE MERE
CUSTODIANS OF THEIR CHILDREN

J esus declared Himself as the way, the truth, and the life (John 14:6). As humans, we often stumble in darkness, searching for meaning and purpose. Yet, by looking to Jesus, we discover the true significance of human existence.

His life provides a blueprint for how we ought to live—a stark contrast to the flawed patterns of behaviour we inherit from Adam. Just as we naturally adopt Adam's sinful nature, we are called to intentionally adopt the ways of Jesus.

Joseph and Mary, the earthly parents of Jesus, played a crucial role in His early life. They protected and nurtured Him as an infant, but as Jesus grew, their influence over His destiny diminished. By the age of twelve, Jesus was already aware of His divine mission and identity.

When His parents found Him in the temple, He said, *"Why were you searching for me? Didn't you know I had to be in my Father's house?"* (Luke 2:49, NIV). This response reveals a profound truth: earthly parents are not the ultimate authority over their children's lives—they are merely custodians.

The Custodial Role of Parents

In the natural order, children often adopt the characteristics, values, and even the religious identities of their parents. Parents teach their children to conform to earthly identities—ethnic, cultural, or denominational.

However, Jesus revealed a higher truth: earthly identities are temporary, but our divine identity in Christ is eternal. Jesus declared Himself as the way, the truth, and the life, em-

103

phasizing that true life is found not in our earthly lineage but in our connection to God.

At twelve years old, Jesus demonstrated that His primary allegiance was to His Heavenly Father, not His earthly parents. This challenges the traditional view that parents have ultimate authority over their children's spiritual lives. While parents are responsible for their children's physical and emotional well-being, they cannot control their spiritual destiny. This is a radical departure from the norm, where children are often pressured to follow their parents' religious traditions or lifestyles.

The Trap of Traditional Christianity

Traditional Christianity often emphasizes the importance of parental authority, sometimes at the expense of a child's personal relationship with God. If parents are Catholic, their children are expected to be Catholic. If parents are Protestant, their children are expected to follow suit.

This approach overlooks the biblical truth that each individual must come to know God personally. Jesus Himself said, *"Call no one on earth your father, for you have one Father, who is in heaven"* (Matthew 23:9, NIV). This statement underscores the importance of direct connection to God, free from human intermediaries.

Christian parents, if truly committed to Christ, must recognize that their children are not their own. They are gifts from God, entrusted to their care for a time. Parents are called to guide their children toward God, not to control their spiritual journey. This requires humility and a willingness to release their children into God's hands, trusting Him to shape their destinies.

The Radical Call of Discipleship

Jesus' teachings often challenged societal norms, especially regarding family relationships. He said, *"If anyone comes to me and does not hate father and mother, wife and children, brothers and sisters—yes, even their own life—such a person cannot be my disciple"* (Luke 14:26, NIV). This statement is not a call to literal hatred but a radical reordering of priorities. Jesus must come first, above all earthly relationships.

This principle applies to parenting as well. Christian parents must prioritize their commitment to Christ over their desire to control or influence their children. This does not mean neglecting their responsibilities but rather recognizing that their role is custodial, not ultimate. They are to model Christ-like behaviour, teach biblical truths, and pray for their children, but they must also allow their children the freedom to choose God for themselves.

The Challenge of Raising Children in Christ

Raising children in a Christ-centred home is a profound responsibility, but it is not without challenges. Christian parents must navigate the tension between guiding their children and allowing them the freedom to make their own decisions. This requires wisdom, patience, and a deep reliance on God.

Parents must also resist the temptation to conform to societal expectations. Many Christian parents worry more about what others think of their parenting than what God thinks. They may pressure their children to conform to religious traditions or denominational practices, rather than encouraging them to develop a personal relationship with Jesus.

This approach often leads to rebellion or a superficial faith. Instead, Christian parents should focus on creating an environment where their children can encounter God's love and truth. They should teach their children to seek God's will above all else and to live as citizens of His Kingdom, not of this world. This means modelling a life of faith, humility, and obedience to Christ.

The Ultimate Goal: Surrendering to God's Will

The ultimate goal of Christian parenting is not to produce perfect children but to point them toward a perfect Saviour. Parents must recognize that their children's spiritual journey is ultimately between them and God. While parents can plant seeds of faith, it is God who brings the growth (1 Corinthians 3:6).

This perspective frees parents from the burden of trying to control their children's destinies. It also reminds them that their primary role is to reflect Christ's love and truth, trusting God to work in their children's lives.

As the apostle Paul wrote, *"Children are a heritage from the Lord, offering a reward from him"* (Psalm 127:3, NIV). Parents are stewards of this precious gift, but the ultimate authority belongs to God.

Practical Steps for Christian Parents

Model Christ-like Behaviour: Children learn more from what they see than from what they are told. Live a life of faith, integrity, and love that reflects Christ.

Teach Biblical Truths: Regularly share Scripture and biblical principles with your children, helping them understand God's Word and His will.

Pray for Your Children: Intercede for your children daily, asking God to guide them and draw them closer to Him.

Release Control: Trust God with your children's futures. Allow them the freedom to make their own decisions and learn from their mistakes.

Encourage Personal Faith: Help your children develop a personal relationship with Jesus, rather than relying on your faith or traditions.

Conclusion: Trusting God with Our Children

Earthly parents are custodians, not owners, of their children. Their role is to nurture, guide, and protect, but the ultimate authority belongs to God. By surrendering their children to Him, parents can find peace and confidence, knowing that He is in control.

Jesus' life and teachings remind us that our true identity is found in Him, not in our earthly relationships or traditions. As Christian parents, we are called to reflect this truth in our parenting, pointing our children toward the One who is the way, the truth, and the life. In doing so, we fulfil our custodial role and honour the God who entrusts us with His precious gifts.

CHAPTER 22

FELLOWSHIP WITH FOCUS

H umans, like animals, naturally seek security and identity through groups. This instinct is deeply rooted in our need for belonging and protection. However, the story of the Tower of Babel reveals the dangers of groupthink and self-centred ambition (Genesis 11:4-8).

In contrast, Jesus modelled a radically different approach to community:

"The Son of Man did not come to be served, but to serve, and to give his life as a ransom for many" (Matthew 20:28, NIV).

True Christians are called to serve others and contribute to the common good, rather than seeking personal advantage through group affiliations. While unity can promote security, ultimate security is found in drawing closer to God.

The builders of Babel sought to make a name for themselves, disregarding God's will. Their unity became a tool for rebellion rather than righteousness.

The Danger of Groupthink

Groupthink often stifles individual reasoning, leading people to accept majority opinions as sacrosanct, even when they conflict with God's principles. Large groups can also dilute genuine affection and love, as resources and attention become limited. Yet, fellowship among believers is encouraged (Hebrews 10:25).

The benefits of fellowship include mutual encouragement, shared wisdom, and collective strength to overcome challenges. However, transitioning from a self-centred mindset to one of altruism is difficult. The Holy Spirit equips believers to live selflessly, fostering unity and love within the body of Christ.

The Church as a Microcosm of God's Kingdom

A church is a microcosm of God's Kingdom. Its foundation was laid by twelve disciples from diverse backgrounds, united by their faith in Christ. The purpose of belonging to a church is not merely for social or emotional security but to grow in faith and service to others.

The authority of Jesus must never be replaced by denominational doctrines or human traditions. True Christians focus on giving—whether through acts of service, listening, or encouraging others. No one takes credit for God's work; all glory belongs to Him.

Embracing Diversity and Tolerance

Christianity embraces diversity, calling believers to coexist peacefully despite differences. Those who cannot tolerate or love unconditionally often separate themselves, as darkness flees from light (1 John 2:19).

Christian fellowship is not about self-centeredness but about mutual edification. Understanding doctrinal truths ahead of others does not justify separation. Sadly, division has plagued Christianity since its early days.

The Example of Jesus

Jesus sought to transform the Jewish community from within, even when it led to His crucifixion. Similarly, believers gifted with discernment should patiently guide others, praying for their spiritual growth rather than withdrawing in frustration.

A true Christian bears responsibility for the misunderstandings of others, reflecting Christ's love for humanity (1 John 3:16). Hiding God's revelations out of fear demonstrates cowardice, which contradicts the purpose of fellowship. Love casts out fear, enabling believers to stand firm in truth, even when facing death.

Humility and Growth

A Christian does not fear suffering or embarrassment when proven wrong. Humility allows us to admit mistakes and grow without shame. Only pride resists correction, while genuine faith embraces truth, even when it challenges our assumptions.

The Holy Spirit empathizes with human limitations; much like a skilled advocate listens to a client's struggles. Likewise, Christians are called to tolerate one another's shortcomings, recognizing the power of unity in achieving God's purposes.

The Tower of Babel and Its Lessons

However, unity can also have drawbacks, as seen in the Tower of Babel. The builders sought to make a name for themselves, but God intervened, scattering them and confusing their language (Genesis 11:4-8). Their concentration in one location would have led to their ultimate demise.

Why did God oppose their unity? Their ambition was rooted in self-glorification, not in serving God or others. Today, nations and groups often compete for dominance, fostering idolatry, favouritism, and conflict. Such divisions lead to wars, resource hoarding, and the spread of contagious diseases.

Jesus' Mission to Reverse Self-Centeredness

Jesus came to reverse the self-centred civilization symbolized by the Tower of Babel. Human groups often fail to consider the negative consequences of their actions, such as alienating others or exploiting resources. Unlike God, who creates something out of nothing, humans often take from others to survive.

The survival of one species often threatens another, reflecting the brokenness of the natural world. Humans, created in God's image, are called to rise above this cycle. Loving our enemies and creating harmony from discord reflects God's nature and sets us apart from the animal kingdom. The purpose of fellowship among Christians is to instil a culture of tolerance and love.

The Great Commission and the Call to Serve

Christians are commissioned to preach the gospel to all nations (Mark 16:15). The persistence of evil in the world, even among believers, reveals the ongoing need for this mission. Self-centeredness and group pride hinder the spread of the gospel.

While fellowship is essential, it must not become inward-focused. Jesus said, *"For where two or three gather in my name, there am I with them"* (Matthew 18:20, NIV).

The goal of fellowship is not to build a name for a denomination or construct impressive buildings but to advance the gospel and serve others. The focus should always be to access the disadvantaged communities.

The Danger of Pride in Fellowship

Elaborate church buildings can unintentionally foster pride, leading believers to compare themselves favourably with others. This mirrors the mindset of the Tower of Babel builders. True fellowship avoids such pitfalls, focusing instead on reaching those outside the faith.

Jesus died for all people, including those considered outsiders or sinners. Light is commonly most effective in darkness, not in places already illuminated. Christians are called to go where the need is greatest, sharing God's love with those struggling in sin.

The Ultimate Goal: Drawing Closer to God

Belonging to a group offers comfort and a sense of belonging. The attractive aspects of this are the fear of exclusion and the pride fostered by like-minded individuals. God's will takes precedence over denominational pride and security concerns. The ultimate goal of fellowship is to draw closer to God, as David expressed.

111

"One thing I ask from the Lord, this only do I seek: that I may dwell in the house of the Lord all the days of my life, to gaze on the beauty of the Lord and to seek him in his temple" (Psalm 27:4, NIV).

Christian fellowship should reflect God's love and inclusivity, embracing people from all backgrounds. Each believer represents Christ's authority, called to promote the values of His Kingdom. By fostering unity, tolerance, and love, Christians can advance the New Civilization that Jesus inaugurated.

Additional Reflections

The Role of Accountability in Fellowship: True fellowship involves holding one another accountable in love. This means gently correcting and encouraging each other to grow in faith (Galatians 6:1-2). Accountability fosters spiritual maturity and prevents the group from drifting into complacency or error.

The Power of Small Groups: While large gatherings have their place, small groups often provide a more intimate setting for deep relationships and spiritual growth. Jesus Himself invested deeply in a small group of disciples, modelling the importance of close, intentional fellowship.

Fellowship as a Witness to the World: When believers live in unity and love, they become a powerful witness to the world. Jesus prayed for this unity, saying, *"May they be brought to complete unity to let the world know that you sent me and have loved them even as you have loved me"* (John 17:23, NIV).

The Balance of Inward and Outward Focus: Fellowship should balance inward care for one another with outward mission to the world. A healthy church community nurtures its members while actively engaging in evangelism and service.

CHAPTER 23

IDOLATRY: THE WORSHIP OF SELF AND FALSE GODS

I dolatry, at its core, is the worship of anything or anyone other than the one true God. It involves elevating a created thing—whether a physical object, a person, or even an idea—to the place of ultimate reverence and devotion.

In the Abrahamic faiths—Judaism, Christianity, and Islam—idolatry is considered a grave sin, a betrayal of the fundamental commandment to worship God alone. Yet, idolatry is not always as obvious as bowing before a statue. Often, it manifests in subtler forms, such as the worship of self, wealth, power, or tradition.

The roots of idolatry can be traced back to the very beginning of human history, to Cain, the first son of Adam. Cain's story is a profound example of how idolatry begins in the heart, long before it is expressed in action. His jealousy and anger toward his brother Abel reveal a heart that had already placed itself above God.

Cain and Abel: A Tale of Two Offerings

The story of Cain and Abel is not merely about sibling rivalry; it is a lesson in worship and the dangers of misplaced priorities. Both brothers brought offerings to God, but their attitudes could not have been more different:

"Now Abel kept flocks, and Cain worked the soil. In the course of time, Cain brought some of the fruits of the soil as an offering to the Lord. And Abel also brought an offering—fat portions from some of the firstborn of his flock. The Lord looked with favour on Abel and his offering, but on Cain and his offering, he did not

look with favour. So Cain was very angry, and his face was downcast" (Genesis 4:2-5, NIV).

At first glance, it may seem unfair that God accepted Abel's offering but rejected Cain's. However, the key lies not in the offerings themselves but in the hearts of those who presented them. Abel gave the best of what he had—the firstborn of his flock and their fat portions—a symbol of his gratitude and reverence for God. Cain, on the other hand, brought "some of the fruits," a gesture that lacked the same intentionality and devotion. Cain's anger revealed his true motive: he sought God's approval for his own sake, not out of genuine love or worship.

His offering was not about honouring God but about elevating himself. In this way, Cain's idolatry was not directed at a physical idol but at his own ego. He had placed himself above God, and his jealousy toward Abel was a symptom of this deeper spiritual ailment.

The Sin at the Door

God, in His mercy, warned Cain about the danger of his attitude: *"Why are you angry? Why is your face downcast? If you do what is right, will you not be accepted? But if you do not do what is right, sin is crouching at your door; it desires to have you, but you must rule over it" (Genesis 4:6-7, NIV).*

Cain's failure to heed this warning led to the first murder in human history. His story is a sobering reminder that idolatry, when left unchecked, leads to destruction. It begins in the heart, with the subtle elevation of self over God, and it ends in chaos and separation from God's will.

The Modern Face of Idolatry

While few today bow before physical idols, idolatry remains a pervasive issue. It takes on new forms, often disguised as ambition, success, or even religious zeal. Consider the following examples:

[Idolatry: The worship of Self and False Gods]

The Idolatry of Success: Many people today worship at the altar of achievement. They measure their worth by their career accomplishments, social status, or financial success. Like Cain, they seek validation and approval, not from God, but from the world around them. This pursuit often leads to discontent, anxiety, and a sense of emptiness.

The Idolatry of Tradition: In religious circles, tradition can become an idol when it takes precedence over the living Word of God. Jesus confronted this issue when He rebuked the Pharisees: *"You have let go of the commands of God and are holding on to human traditions" (Mark 7:8, NIV)*. Traditions, while valuable, must never overshadow the transformative power of the gospel.

The Idolatry of Self: Perhaps the most insidious form of idolatry is the worship of self. This manifests in pride, self-reliance, and a desire for control. Like Cain, many today are driven by their egos, seeking to elevate themselves above others—and even above God.

Jesus and the Call to Self-Denial

Jesus addressed the root of idolatry when He called His followers to deny themselves and take up their cross:

"Then Jesus said to his disciples, 'Whoever wants to be my disciple must deny themselves and take up their cross and follow me'" (Matthew 16:24, NIV).

This call to self-denial is a direct challenge to the idolatry of self. It requires us to relinquish our desire for control, recognition, and comfort, and to submit fully to God's will. Jesus exemplified this in the Garden of Gethsemane when He prayed, *"My Father, if it is possible, may this cup be taken from me. Yet not as I will, but as you will" (Matthew 26:39, NIV)*. In this moment of anguish, Jesus demonstrated the ultimate act of surrender, but choosing God's will over His own.

The Danger of Spiritual Idolatry

Even in religious practices, idolatry can creep in. Jesus warned against those who perform acts of worship for show or personal gain:

"Not everyone who says to me, 'Lord, Lord,' will enter the kingdom of heaven, but only the one who does the will of my Father who is in heaven. Many will say to me on that day, 'Lord, Lord, did we not prophesy in your name and in your name drive out demons and in your name perform many miracles?' Then I will tell them plainly, 'I never knew you. Away from me, you evildoers!'" (Matthew 7:21-23, NIV).

These individuals may appear righteous, but their motives are tainted by self-interest. They seek recognition and reward, not the glory of God. This is idolatry in its most deceptive form.

Practical Steps to Overcome Idolatry

1. **Examine Your Heart**: Ask yourself, "What or who do I value most? Where do I seek validation and fulfilment?" Be honest about the things that compete with God for your devotion.
2. **Practice Self-Denial**: Follow Jesus' example by surrendering your desires and ambitions to God. Seek His will above your own, even when it requires sacrifice.
3. **Cultivate Gratitude**: Like Abel, offer God the best of what you have, not out of obligation, but out of a heart of gratitude and love.
4. **Renew Your Mind**: As Paul writes, *"Do not conform to the pattern of this world, but be transformed by the renewing of your mind" (Romans 12:2, NIV).* Fill your mind with God's Word and allow it to shape your priorities and actions.

Conclusion: Worship God Alone

Idolatry, in all its forms, is a rejection of God's sovereignty and a distortion of true worship. It leads to emptiness, conflict, and separation from God. Yet, through Jesus, we have the power to overcome idolatry. By denying ourselves, taking up our cross, and following Him, we can break free from the chains of self-worship and live in alignment with God's will.

Let us heed the warning of Cain's story and the call of Jesus. Let us worship God alone, offering Him our hearts, our lives, and our very best. In doing so, we will find true fulfilment and the abundant life that only He can provide.

CHAPTER 24

CHRISTIANS SHOULDN'T AVOID CONFRONTING SPIRITS

The concept of spirits is deeply rooted in African traditions, yet it remains a contentious topic in Christianity. In Ndebele, the correct translation of "spirit" is idhlozi, while in Shona, it is mudzimu. However, many Christians avoid these vernacular terms, preferring translations like Mweya Mutsvene (Shona) or, uMoya Oyingcwele (Ndebele) for the Holy Spirit.
These translations, while widely used, are linguistically and theologically inaccurate. Mweya and uMoya refer to breath or the wind that blows, not the spiritual essence conveyed by idhlozi or, mudzimu, (Shona).
This mistranslation reflects a broader issue: the reluctance of Christians to engage with the spiritual realm, particularly as understood in African traditions.

The Disconnect Between Christianity and African Spirituality

Early missionaries, in their efforts to spread Christianity, often discouraged African converts from engaging with their ancestral traditions. They viewed African spirituality as incompatible with Christian teachings, labelling it as demonic or superstitious.
This approach was not only dismissive but also counterproductive. By rejecting African spiritual concepts, missionaries created a false dichotomy between Christianity and African spirituality as it linked with their cultural identity. The dichotomy ought to be limited to good and evil, instead.
For example, the missionaries' insistence on using Mweya Mutsvene instead of Mudzimu Mutvene (Holy Spir-

it) reflects a deliberate attempt to distance African Christians from their ancestral heritage.

This linguistic shift was not merely semantic; it was a theological and cultural imposition that alienated Africans from their spiritual roots.

Missionaries aimed to help Africans appreciate Jesus by separating them from their spiritual traditions. However, a more effective approach would have been to help them understand how their spirituality connected with the God of the Bible.

While the ancient religions of Europe promoted mythology and idolatry, Africans were connected with God through their ancestral spirits. Like everyone, they needed salvation, but they had a proper understanding of the significance of spirituality.

The Superiority of the Spiritual Realm

Spiritual beings, whether good or evil, operate on a plane that transcends physical reality. This is a truth that both African traditions and Christianity affirm. In the Bible, Jesus frequently confronted spirits, demonstrating their reality and power. For instance, when Jesus encountered a man possessed by demons, the spirits recognized Him immediately:

"What do you want with us, Son of God?" they shouted. "Have you come here to torture us before the appointed time?" (Matthew 8:29, NIV).

This interaction highlights two key points:

1) **Spirits are real and powerful**: They possess knowledge and abilities beyond human understanding.
2) **Jesus has authority over all spirits**: His power is unmatched, and He empowers His followers to confront and overcome spiritual forces.

Despite this biblical precedent, many Christians today shy away from engaging with the spiritual realm. They dismiss

African ancestral spirits (amadlozi/midzimu) as irrelevant or demonic, failing to recognize that spirits, in general, are a reality that must be confronted, not ignored.

The Fear of Spirits and Witchcraft

One reason Christians avoid confronting spirits is fear. Witchcraft, for example, is often treated as a taboo subject, spoken of in hushed tones but rarely addressed directly. This fear stems from a lack of understanding and spiritual authority. Many Christians are unaware of their God-given power to confront and overcome spiritual forces. Jesus explicitly promised His followers authority over spirits:

"And these signs will accompany those who believe: In my name, they will drive out demons; they will speak in new tongues; they will pick up snakes with their hands; and when they drink deadly poison, it will not hurt them at all; they will place their hands on sick people, and they will get well" (Mark 16:17-18, NIV).

This promise is not limited to a select few but extends to all believers. Yet, many Christians fail to exercise this authority, allowing fear and ignorance to dominate their approach to spiritual matters. Failure to confront demonic spirit is a result of lacking sincerity in one's spiritual condition.

The Role of Ancestral Spirits in African Tradition

In African traditions, ancestral spirits (amadlozi/midzimu) are seen as intermediaries between the living and the divine. They are not inherently evil but are respected and honoured for their wisdom and guidance.

However, when these spirits are misunderstood or misrepresented, they can become sources of fear and confusion. For example, King Saul, a prominent figure in the Bible, consulted a spirit medium when he felt abandoned by God (1 Samuel 28:3-25).

This story illustrates the human tendency to seek guidance from spiritual sources, even when it contradicts divine principles. While Saul's actions were condemned, the narrative acknowledges the reality of spirits and their influence.

The Need for Spiritual Discernment

Christians must develop spiritual discernment to navigate the complexities of the spiritual realm. This involves:

Recognizing the reality of spirits: Both good and evil spirits exist and influence the physical world.

Exercising authority in Christ: Believers have the power to confront and overcome spiritual forces through faith in Jesus.

Rejecting fear and superstition: Fear is a tool of the enemy, but faith in Christ brings victory over all spiritual opposition.

Practical Steps for Confronting Spirits

Prayer and Fasting: These spiritual disciplines strengthen believers and equipping them to confront spiritual forces in their demonic patterns (Matthew 17:21).

Scriptural Authority: The Bible is a powerful weapon against spiritual opposition (Matthew 4:3-11 & Ephesians 6:17).

Community Support: Believers should support one another in spiritual battles, praying and standing together in faith.

Conclusion: Embracing Spiritual Authority

Christians must not avoid confronting spirits, as Jesus said they would have authority over them. Instead, they should embrace their God-given authority to engage with the spiritual realm. By understanding and respecting African spiritual concepts, Christians can bridge the gap between faith and culture, demonstrating the supremacy of Christ over all spiritual forces.

Jesus' victory over sin, death, and the powers of darkness is the foundation of our faith. As His followers, we are called to walk in that victory, confronting spirits with confidence and authority. Let us move beyond fear and ignorance, embracing the fullness of our spiritual heritage in Christ.

CHAPTER 25

CHRISTIANITY AND
FAMILY MEMBERS

I t is rare for an individual to embrace Christianity alongside their entire family, unless it is adopted as a cultural or traditional practice. More often than not, Christianity is a solitary journey—one that demands a transformed lifestyle, often without the agreement or understanding of those closest to us.

This is why Jesus emphasized the sacrificial nature of following Him (Matthew 19:29). Accepting Christ brings a profound sense of joy and a new perspective on life, but it can also create tension with family members who do not share the same faith.

A Christian is called to love even their enemies—a directive that seems impractical to the secular mind. Consider, too, the call to missions or other commitments that may appear unreasonable to one's immediate family.

From a human perspective, Christianity can seem unworkable, as it often strains familial bonds. The principles of harmonious relationships, particularly in marriage, do not always align with the demands of Christian discipleship. This is perhaps why Paul recommended celibacy as a preferable state for some (1 Corinthians 7:7-8).

Jesus Himself called for the prioritization of spiritual commitments over family ties, a teaching that may seem at odds with passages like Proverbs 18:22, which celebrates the blessings of marriage, yet, there is no contradiction.

A Christian is a new creation (2 Corinthians 5:17), fundamentally different from the person described in Proverbs 18:22. While many Christians enjoy healthy marriages, such relationships do not necessarily indicate spiritual superiority. This is one reason why Christ cautioned against judgment (Matthew 7:1-5; James 4:11-12).

Human understanding is limited, and even within Christian marriages, doctrinal differences can lead to significant challenges. For instance, one spouse may observe the Sabbath as a sacred commandment, while the other may believe they are no longer bound by such laws. These differences are not always resolved through explanation, as truth is often a deeply personal conviction.

Even Jesus did not rely solely on Scripture to win converts. What is true for one person may not resonate with another, and vice versa. This is where the principle of respecting differing viewpoints becomes essential. Christ taught that no one comes to Him unless drawn by the Father (John 6:44).

However, if both spouses heed Paul's advice in Romans 14—to avoid quarrelling over disputable matters—such conflicts can be managed. A true believer is led by the Spirit, not by societal norms or traditions.

Repentance is a deeply personal and qualitative experience. Doctrinal differences, as Paul noted, should not interfere with one's convictions. Christ meets people where they are, perfecting them according to their unique circumstances rather than rigid doctrinal frameworks.

Unbelievers are not enemies but spiritual strangers. It is wise to avoid unnecessary debates over biblical matters unless explicitly invited to share one's perspective. Engaging others in Bible study is commendable, but only when they are open and willing. The primary goal is to preach Christ, but this must be done in a spirit of peace and respect.

When Jesus sent His disciples on their mission, He instructed them to first seek peace in every household they entered (Luke 10:5). The most effective way to share the gospel is through respectful dialogue and genuine love. Peter's advice to wives with unbelieving husbands—and by extension, to husbands with unbelieving wives—is instructive:

"Wives, in the same way, submit yourselves to your own husbands so that, if any of them do not believe the word, they may be won over without words by the behaviour of their wives" (1 Peter 3:1, NIV).

Paul's approach also offers valuable insight. He adapted his methods to connect with different audiences, becoming "all things to all people" to win some for Christ (1 Corinthians 9:19-23). Conflicts may also arise with extended family, particularly when Christian convictions lead to the refusal of certain cultural or ritual practices. Such decisions can result in ostracism or misunderstanding, as Jesus Himself warned:

"Do not suppose that I have come to bring peace to the earth. I did not come to bring peace, but a sword. For I have come to turn 'a man against his father, a daughter against her mother, a daughter-in-law against her mother-in-law—a man's enemies will be the members of his own household'" (Matthew 10:34-36, NIV).

While this passage paints a stark picture of familial discord, it is not a call to provoke conflict. Rather, it prepares believers for the challenges that may arise as they live out their faith. Being hated or misunderstood by relatives is not an excuse to respond in kind. Christianity calls for love even in the face of hostility. Persecutors need love more than ever, and difficult circumstances provide opportunities to demonstrate the transformative power of Christ's teachings.

Without such trials, it would be impossible to develop the character and resilience necessary for a godly life. This love is not rooted in doctrinal correctness but in empathy for those who do not yet understand the truth. Spiritual matters must always take precedence over physical concerns, as Jesus demonstrated when He prioritized His spiritual family over His biological relatives:

"Then Jesus' mother and brothers arrived. Standing outside, they sent someone in to call Him. A crowd was sitting around Him, and they told Him, 'Your mother and brothers are outside looking for You.' 'Who are My mother and My brothers?' He asked. Then He looked at those seated in a circle around Him and said, 'Here are My mother and My brothers! Whoever does God's will is My brother and sister and mother'" (Mark 3:31-35, NIV).

To Jesus, those who embraced the gospel were of greater value than even His closest earthly relatives. This underscores the eternal significance of spiritual relationships over temporary, earthly ties. Similarly, when a disciple asked to bury his father before following Jesus, the Lord replied:

"Follow Me, and let the dead bury their own dead" (Matthew 8:22, NIV).

This statement highlights the spiritual reality that without Christ, a person is spiritually dead. Physical death is merely the culmination of a life already separated from God. The unconverted have hope, however, Christ's sacrifice is inclusive, as illustrated in the parable of the lost sheep (Luke 15:1-7).

Those who respond to His call are of immeasurable value, even as He continues to seek the lost. Marriage, too, presents unique challenges for believers, particularly when one spouse is unconverted. Yet, Jesus affirmed the sanctity of marriage, stating that what God has joined together, no one should separate (Matthew 19:6).

While an unequally yoked marriage may seem disadvantageous, it is not beyond God's redemptive power. Just as Moses overcame his speech impediment to lead Israel, God can use even the most challenging circumstances for His glory.

Loving an unlovable spouse or family member fosters the development of godly a character. God loved humanity while we were still sinners, and Christians are called to emulate this unconditional love. A minister in a difficult marriage can still be effective in their calling, for God's approval matters more than human approval. Misusing Scripture to justify divorce or discord contradicts the spirit of Christ's teachings.

Paul's admonition against being unequally yoked (2 Corinthians 6:14-16) is often misinterpreted in the context of marriage. However, it primarily refers to partnerships in ministry, not marital unions. In God's kingdom, marriage is a temporary institution (Matthew 22:30), but while on earth, believers are called to honour their commitments.

Avoiding unnecessary disputes over biblical interpretations is wise. Even when convinced of one's understanding, truth should never be imposed. Instead, believers should seek peace and treat others as they would like to be treated (Matthew 7:12). Christians are called to be as wise as serpents and as harmless as doves (Matthew 10:16), navigating relationships with grace and humility.

Ultimately, the effectiveness of Christianity is measured not by human approval but by faithfulness to God. By loving others as Christ loves us and offering guidance only when sought, believers can build bridges rather than walls.

The family can be the first testing ground for these principles. When love triumphs over discord, even in the most challenging environments, the transformative power of Christianity becomes evident. This is the true essence of Christian fellowship.

CHAPTER 26

CHURCH LEADERSHIP

" Therefore, whoever humbles himself as this little child is the greatest in the kingdom of heaven... But whoever causes one of these little ones who believe in me to stumble, it would be better for him to have a huge millstone hung around his neck and to be drowned in the depth of the sea!" (Matthew 18:1-7, EMTV).

Jesus' response to the disciples' question about greatness in the Kingdom of Heaven reveals a radical redefinition of leadership. In a world that often equates leadership with power, prestige, and privilege, Jesus calls His followers to embrace humility, servant-hood, and childlike faith, so that each believer remains willing to learn at all times. This chapter explores the nature of church leadership, its responsibilities, and the dangers of misusing authority.

The Call to Humility

Jesus' teaching on humility challenges the conventional understanding of leadership. He elevates the status of a child, symbolizing innocence, dependence, and humility, as the model for greatness in God's Kingdom. This stands in stark contrast to the world's emphasis on titles, achievements, and hierarchical structures.

Church leaders are called to serve, not to be served. Their authority is not for personal gain but for the edification of the body of Christ. As Jesus warned, causing "one of these little ones" to stumble carries severe consequences. The imagery of a millstone—a heavy stone used for grinding grain—symbolizes the weight of responsibility and the gravity of leading others astray.

The Danger of Causing Stumbling

Jesus' warning about the millstone underscores the seriousness of leadership accountability. Leaders who misuse their authority, promote false teachings, or foster division risk leading others into spiritual harm. This is not just a caution for pastors or elders but for anyone in a position of influence within the church.

As bearing multifaceted gifts of the Holy Spirit, each Christian, among various brethren, carries some responsibility of leadership. The consequences of causing others to stumble are twofold:

For the Leader: The millstone represents irreversible condemnation, highlighting the eternal stakes of leadership. The error is in allowing others to use one as the authority, thereby leading them astray. Otherwise, Christian leadership is exclusively vested on Jesus Christ, according to what was pronounced by Jesus in Matthew 23:1-8.

For the Follower: Those led astray face spiritual peril, emphasizing the need for leaders to shepherd with integrity and care. This requires each follower to check whether what is said agrees with the teachings of Jesus.

The Role of Leaders in the Church

Paul outlines various roles within the church, as summarized in Ephesians 4:11:

"And He Himself gave some to be apostles, some prophets, some evangelists, and some pastors and teachers."

These roles are not hierarchical but functional, each contributing to the growth and unity of the body of Christ. Let's examine each role in detail:

1. Apostles

The term "apostle" means "one who is sent." The original apostles were eyewitnesses of Christ's ministry and resurrection, tasked with laying the foundation of the church. However, their authority was not derived from their position but from their faithfulness to Christ's mission.

Modern-day apostles (if such a role exists) would similarly focus on pioneering new works, planting churches, and equipping believers.

Their role is not to dominate but to serve, ensuring that the gospel reaches every corner of the world. However, when purely guided by Scripture, the term "Apostles" was exclusive to the designated twelve disciples:

Now it came to pass in those days that He went out to the mountain to pray, and continued all night in prayer to God. And when it was day, He called His disciples to Himself; and from them He chose twelve whom He also named apostles (Luke 6:12-13 NKJV).

2. Prophets

Prophets are not merely predictors of the future but revealers of God's truth. They speak to strengthen, encourage, and comfort the church (1 Corinthians 14:3). While some prophets may receive divine revelations, their primary role is to edify the body of Christ.

Prophecy is a spiritual gift, not a mark of superiority. As Paul reminds us, *"We know in part and we prophesy in part"* (1 Corinthians 13:9). Prophets must operate with humility, recognizing the limitations of their understanding and the supremacy of Christ.

3. Evangelists

Evangelists are heralds of the gospel, called to spread the good news of salvation. Their role is not confined to pulpit ministry but extends to everyday interactions, sharing Christ's love with those who do not yet know Him.

The Great Commission (Matthew 28:19-20) is a mandate for all believers, not just evangelists. However, those gifted in evangelism often lead the charge, inspiring and equipping others to share their faith. Based on the instruction on the Great Commission all believers are equipped with the responsibility to evangelize.

4. Pastors

The term "pastor" comes from the Greek word for "shepherd." Pastors are called to care for the flock, protecting them from false teachings and guiding them toward spiritual maturity. Their role is not to lord over others but to serve as examples of Christ's love and humility (1 Peter 5:2-3).

Their activities are patterned according to Jesus' teachings and actions. Jesus is the ultimate Shepherd (John 10:11), and pastors are merely under-shepherds, entrusted with the care of His sheep.

Their authority is derived from Christ, not from their title or position. They undertake to serve similarly to how Jesus Christ served, ensuring the flock is selflessly looked after and protected from false doctrines.

5. Teachers

Teachers play a crucial role in the church, helping believers understand and apply God's Word. Their gift is not for personal acclaim but for the edification of the body.

As James warns, *"Not many of you should become teachers, my fellow believers, because you know that we who teach will be judged more strictly"* (James 3:1, NIV).

Teachers must handle Scripture with care, ensuring that their instruction aligns with the truth of the gospel. Teachers may not necessarily be pastors or holding any other responsibility, although possible for any person to be gifted with multifaceted gifts in God's Church.

[Church Leadership]

The Danger of Pride in Leadership

Pride is a constant threat to church leaders. The adulation of admirers, the success of ministerial endeavours, and the temptation to compare oneself with others can all lead to spiritual downfall. As Proverbs 16:18 warns, *"Pride goes before destruction, a haughty spirit before a fall."*

Leaders must remain vigilant, guarding their hearts against pride and relying on the Holy Spirit for guidance and strength. It is worth noting that the adulation from fellow brethren can easily tempt an otherwise gifted individual to become proud. Congregations, too, have a role to play by praying for their leaders and holding them accountable in love.

The Equality of All Believers

While leadership roles are essential, they do not elevate individuals above others within the body of Christ. Paul underscores the unity and equality of all believers, likening the church to a body with many parts (1 Corinthians 12:12-31). Each member has a unique role to fulfil, and no role is more important than another.

The so-called "laymen" are not second-class citizens in the church. Every believer is called to serve, using their gifts for the glory of God and the good of the body. Titles and positions are secondary to the call to love and serve one another.

Each church member carries some responsibility that is often suppressed due to the paternalistic approach for which Christianity has become known. Paul attests to the equality of all brethren, regardless of background and gender (Galatians 3:26-29).

Practical Implications for Church Leadership

Servant Leadership: Leaders must model Christ's humility, prioritizing the needs of others above their own.
Accountability: Leaders should surround themselves with trusted individuals who can provide wise counsel and hold them accountable.

Empowerment: Leaders must equip and empower others to use their gifts, fostering a culture of shared ministry.

Focus on Christ: Leaders must keep Christ at the centre of their ministry, ensuring that all glory goes to Him.

Church leadership is a sacred trust, requiring humility, integrity, and a deep dependence on Christ. Every baptized member of the Church is entrusted with a portion of leadership so that no single person is seen as solely responsible for misleading others.

Leaders are called to serve, not to be served, and to shepherd the flock with love and care. The consequences of misusing authority are severe, but the rewards of faithful leadership are eternal.

As we reflect on the roles and responsibilities of church leaders, let us remember that all authority belongs to Christ. He is the Head of the Church, and we are His body, called to work together in unity and love.

May we strive to lead with humility, serve with joy, and glorify Him in everything we do. Anyone who perceives wrongdoing and does nothing about it abdicates responsibility. Each Christian is responsible for shepherding fellow believers (James 4:17).

CHAPTER 27

CHURCH FINANCING

C hristianity calls us to follow Christ in every aspect of life, including how we approach church financing. Jesus' teachings provide a solid foundation for all we do, and building on this foundation ensures stability and integrity in our practices. As Jesus said, *"Everyone who hears these words of mine and puts them into practice is like a wise man who built his house on the rock"* (Matthew 7:24, NIV).

However, the prosperity gospel—a popular but misguided teaching—emphasizes wealth and material blessings as signs of God's favour. This stands in stark contrast to Jesus' warning: *"Enter through the narrow gate. For wide is the gate and broad is the road that leads to destruction, and many enter through it. But small is the gate and narrow the road that leads to life, and only a few find it"* (Matthew 7:13-14, NIV).

Church financing must align with Christ's teachings, not worldly principles. Jesus declared Himself the builder of His Church (Matthew 16:18), and He alone bears the ultimate responsibility for its growth and sustenance. This chapter explores biblical principles for church financing, the dangers of misaligned motives, and the importance of generosity rooted in love and faith. The common mistake is to be motivated by others to give.

The Church Financing Foundation

Church financing should reflect the values of the Kingdom of God, not the values of the world. Jesus' teachings and example provide the blueprint for how we should approach financial matters in the church.

Freedom in Giving: Under the New Covenant, giving is not a legal obligation but a voluntary act of worship. Paul's instructions to the Corinthians emphasize cheerful and willing giving (2 Corinthians 9:7). Unlike the Old Covenant, where tithing was a legal requirement, the New Covenant encourages generosity motivated by love and gratitude.

Avoiding Hypocrisy: Jesus condemned the Pharisees for their showy acts of giving, which were done to gain human approval rather than to honour God.

He taught, *"When you give to the needy, do not let your left hand know what your right hand is doing, so that your giving may be in secret. Then your Father, who sees what is done in secret, will reward you"* (Matthew 6:3-4, NIV).

Servant Leadership: Church leaders are called to serve, not to exploit their positions for personal gain. Jesus warned against the hypocrisy of the scribes and Pharisees, who burdened others with demands while failing to practice what they preached (Matthew 23:4). Jesus never solicited His disciples to financially support His Ministry. Likewise, it is not the duty of Church leaders to solicit Church financing.

The Danger of Misaligned Motives

Church financing can be driven by two contrasting motives:

Spiritual Motivation: This is rooted in love for God and others. It seeks to advance the Kingdom of God and meet the needs of the church and the community. Financial givers are motivated by the Spirit, rather than by Church leaders and do so anonymously.

Egotistical Motivation: This is rooted in self-interest, greed, or the desire for power and recognition. It often leads to exploitation and undermines the integrity of the church. Such givers are known to attract being conferred with leadership positions, thereby, desecrating the Church of God.

The prosperity gospel, which equates financial success with spiritual favour, is a prime example of misaligned motives. It distorts the true message of the gospel and places undue emphasis on material wealth. Jesus' teachings consistently warn against the love of money and the deceitfulness of wealth (Matthew 6:19-24; Luke 12:15 & 1Timothy 6:3-12).

Biblical Principles for Church Financing

1) *Generosity Rooted in Love:* The early church provides a powerful example of generosity. Believers sold their possessions and shared their resources to meet the needs of the community (Acts 2:44-45; 4:32-35). This was not a legal requirement but a spontaneous response to the love and grace they had received in Christ.

2) *Support for Ministry Workers:* Paul affirmed the right of ministry workers to receive financial support, citing the principle that *"the worker deserves his wages"* (1 Timothy 5:18, NIV). However, this support should be given willingly, not as an obligation or a means of control. Otherwise, it is dishonourable to demand finances from God's children.

3) *Jesus' example:* When sending His disciples for evangelism, Jesus advised them not to carry anything but to rely on what would be provided by strangers who would receive them.

   They were not to solicit funds from strangers, for their needs, except by being fed by the hospitable men of peace (Luke 10:5-7). At that time, the disciples had not yet received the Holy Spirit. In contrast, a spiritually guided Church is financed by those gifted with the ability to give, according to Romans 12:8.

a) *Transparency and Accountability:* Church finances should be managed with integrity and transparency. Leaders must be good stewards of the resources entrusted to them, ensuring that funds are used for their intended purposes (1 Corinthians 4:2).

b) *Focus on Spiritual Priorities:* The primary mission of the church is to preach the gospel and make disciples

(Matthew 28:19-20). Financial resources should be directed toward fulfilling this mission, not toward building personal empires or indulging in extravagance.

A faithful servant of God does not feel dependant on anyone for financing God's projects, hence, according to Jesus, finances are provided anonymously.

The Role of Professionals in the Church

In the secular world, professionals are compensated for their skills and expertise. Similarly, those who serve the church in professional capacities—such as pastors, administrators, and musicians—deserve fair compensation for their work. However, as servants of God, their motivation should be service, not personal gain.

Jesus modelled this principle by serving others selflessly, even laying down His life for humanity. His ministry was not driven by financial incentives but by love and obedience to the Father. Church leaders must follow His example, prioritizing spiritual impact over financial rewards.

The Danger of Fundraising Overemphasis

While fundraising is occasionally necessary, it should never become the primary focus of the church. When the church prioritizes fundraising over spiritual ministry, it risks losing sight of its mission and alienating its members.

God should be regarded as being more aware of the financial needs of those seeking funding for such projects. All funding requests should be directed to God, rather than expecting to be financed by fellow humans.

Instead, the church should focus on providing commendable services that inspire voluntary giving. As Jesus demonstrated, genuine love and service naturally elicit generosity. The widow who gave her last two coins (Luke 21:1-4) was motivated by her love for God, not by external pressure or obligation.

Her giving was sacrificial, rather than calculated according to budgetary concerns. Jesus said she gave more than those rich people who may have given out of pomposity, but assured of sufficient reserves.

The New Covenant Perspective on Wealth

The New Covenant redefines our understanding of wealth and blessings. In the Old Covenant, material prosperity was often seen as a sign of God's favour. In the New Covenant, spiritual riches take precedence over material wealth. Spiritual blessings are not measured by prosperity but by service, as spiritually inspired.

1. **Wealth as a Potential Curse:** Jesus warned that wealth can be a stumbling block to spiritual growth. The parable of the rich man and Lazarus (Luke 16:19-31) illustrates the dangers of placing trust in material possessions rather than in God.

2. **Humility and Servant-hood:** In the New Covenant, leadership is characterized by humility and servant-hood. Jesus taught, *"The greatest among you will be your servant"* (Matthew 23:11, NIV). This principle applies to how leaders should handle church finances. It is only in this world that leaders are served as bosses.

3. **Blessed Are the Poor in Spirit:** Jesus declared, *"Blessed are the poor in spirit, for theirs is the kingdom of heaven"* (Matthew 5:3, NIV). True wealth is found in a humble and dependent relationship with God, not in material abundance. The willingness to learn at all times is what keeps the child of God unwaveringly focused.

Practical Steps for Biblical Church Financing

a) **Teach Biblical Generosity**: Church leaders should teach the principles of cheerful and voluntary giving, emphasizing the joy of contributing to God's work.

b) **Model Integrity and Transparency:** Leaders must handle church finances with integrity, ensuring that resources are used wisely and ethically.

c) **Focus on Spiritual Impact:** Financial decisions should align with the church's mission to preach the gospel and serve the community.

d) **Encourage Anonymous Giving:** To avoid the temptation of seeking recognition, the church should promote anonymous giving, as Jesus taught in Matthew 6:1-4.

Church financing is not merely a practical matter but a spiritual one. It reflects our understanding of God's provision, our commitment to His mission, and our willingness to serve others selflessly. By aligning our financial practices with Christ's teachings, we honour Him and advance His Kingdom.

Let us remember that the church belongs to Christ, and He is its ultimate provider. Our role is to steward His resources with humility, integrity, and love, trusting that He will supply all our needs according to His riches in glory (Philippians 4:19).

CHAPTER 28

PRAYER AND GOD'S WILL

God's will is paramount. Yet, many people fall into super-stition, mistaking their inner feelings or desires for di-vine guidance. To truly understand and align with God's will, we must first appreciate His existence and seek His voice with sincerity and clarity.

Without this foundation, our prayers and actions risk being misguided or even manipulated by spiritual confusion. As Paul writes, *"I have been crucified with Christ, and I no long-er live, but Christ lives in me"* (Galatians 2:20, ASV).

This profound statement reveals that the Christian life is not about pursuing our own desires but surrendering to Christ's will. When Christ lives in us, we experience a foretaste of heaven—a state of spiritual union with Him (Revelation 3:20-21; John 14:1-7, 20-23).

Jesus assured His followers that those who live by faith can overcome even the most daunting challenges: *"Very truly I tell you, whoever believes in me will do the works I have been doing, and they will do even greater things than these"* (John 14:12, NIV).

Yet, despite the abundance of churches and Christian denominations, many still struggle to live out this faith. True Christianity is not measured by the number of churches but by the depth of faith and obedience to God's will.

Understanding God's Will

God's will is not a mystery to be deciphered but a real-ity to be embraced through prayer and obedience. Paul exhorts us, *"Therefore do not be foolish, but understand what the Lord's will is"* (Ephesians 5:17, NIV).

Prayer is the key to aligning our hearts with God's will. Jesus taught His disciples to pray to avoid falling into temptation (Luke 22:40), emphasizing the importance of staying connected to God in every circumstance. Prayer is not about bending God's will to our desires but about submitting our will to His. As James warns, *"When you ask, you do not receive, because you ask with wrong motives, that you may spend what you get on your pleasures"* (James 4:3, NIV). True prayer seeks God's will above all else, trusting that His plans are for our ultimate good (Romans 8:28).

The Model Prayer

When Jesus' disciples asked Him to teach them how to pray, He provided a model that encapsulates the essence of prayer:

"Father, hallowed be your name, your kingdom come. Give us each day our daily bread. Forgive us our sins, for we also forgive everyone who sins against us. And lead us not into temptation" (Luke 11:2-4, NIV).

This prayer, often referred to as the Lord's Prayer, is not a ritual to be repeated mindlessly but a framework for aligning our hearts with God's will. Let's explore the content of its components:

1. "Hallowed Be Your Name"

This petition reminds us to honour and glorify God in all we do. Our lives should reflect His character, setting us apart from the world. When we pray for God's name to be hallowed, we commit to living in a way that brings Him glory.

2. "Your Kingdom Come"

Praying for God's Kingdom to come shifts our focus from earthly concerns to eternal priorities. It reminds us that our ultimate citizenship is in heaven (Philippians 3:20) and challenges us to live as ambassadors of Christ's Kingdom.

3. "Give Us Each Day Our Daily Bread"

This request acknowledges our dependence on God for both physical and spiritual sustenance. It teaches us to trust Him for our daily needs while seeking the "bread of life"—His Word—that nourishes our souls (John 6:35).

4. "Forgive Us Our Sins, for We Also Forgive Everyone Who Sins Against Us"

Forgiveness is central to the Christian life. We cannot expect God's forgiveness while harbouring unforgivingness toward others. As John writes, *"Anyone who does not love their brother and sister, whom they have seen, cannot love God, whom they have not seen"* (1 John 4:20, NIV).

5. "Lead Us Not into Temptation"

While God does not tempt us (James 1:13), Satan can be expected to tempt us daily, except when God answers the preceding four petitions, making the prayer to avoid temptation more manageable.

This petition acknowledges our vulnerability to sin and our need for His guidance. Avoiding temptation while living in the flesh is a daunting task. This is a plea for strength to resist temptation and remain faithful to God.

The Power of Persistent Prayer

Jesus taught the importance of persistent prayer through the parable of the persistent widow (Luke 18:1-8). However, this parable is not about manipulating God to fulfil our desires but about trusting His timing and justice.

Persistent prayer aligns our hearts with God's will, transforming our desires to match His. The most effective way of maintaining God's will is to remain engaged in God's work at all times, so the mind remains focused.

Prayer and Temptation

Prayer is a powerful tool for resisting temptation. When we pray, we invite God's presence and strength into our lives, enabling us to overcome the enemy's schemes. Jesus demonstrated this in the wilderness, where He countered Satan's temptations with Scripture (Matthew 4:1-11).

Fasting, when often paired with prayer, deepens our spiritual focus and dependence on God. The spirit is strengthened when the physical body is weakened. Hence, Jesus said we should celebrate when physically persecuted, rather than when physically blessed (Matthew 5:10-12).

Fasting weakens the flesh, allowing the spirit to thrive. As Jesus taught, some spiritual battles can only be won through prayer and fasting (Matthew 17:21).

The Futility of Self-Sufficiency

Material wealth and self-sufficiency can often lead a Christian away from God. King Solomon, despite his wisdom, drifted from God after accumulating great wealth (1 Kings 11:4). Similarly, those in poverty may struggle to trust God when consumed by physical needs.

Christianity requires appreciating self-sufficiency, even when living in what the world describes as abject poverty. A Christian values being alive today without worrying about tomorrow. Prayer and Bible study help us maintain a balanced perspective, reminding us that true security is found in God alone. This becomes possible and easily manageable when occupied with the work of God at all times.

As Hebrews 13:5-6 assures us, *"Keep your lives free from the love of money and be content with what you have because God has said, 'Never will I leave you; never will I forsake you.' So we say with confidence, 'The Lord is my helper; I will not be afraid. What can mere mortals do to me?'"*

The Plural Nature of Prayer

The Lord's Prayer is written in the plural form, emphasizing our interconnectedness as believers. We are called to bear one another's burdens (Galatians 6:2) and pray for the needs of others, than limiting our prayers to our personal needs only. This communal aspect of prayer reflects the unity of the body of Christ, so that there cannot be any feeling of competition but cooperation.

Prayer is not a means to manipulate God but a way to align our hearts with His will. Through prayer, we surrender our desires, seek His guidance, and find strength to resist temptation. The Lord's Prayer provides a model for this transformative practice, reminding us to honour God, seek His Kingdom, and trust Him for our daily needs.

As we pray, let us remember that God's will is supreme. Our role is not to change His will but to allow Him to change our will to align with His. By embracing His will, we participate in the New Civilization—a restoration of the harmony between humanity and God that was lost in Eden. It is impossible to be a Christian when not aligning with God's will.

CHAPTER 29

TRUE CHRISTIANITY

What does it mean to be a true Christian? This question often elicits a wide range of answers, from avoiding certain foods or habits to strict law-keeping, regular church attendance, or even out-competing other religions. Yet, true Christianity transcends these external practices. It is not about conforming to religious traditions or earning a badge of honour but about embodying the love and character of Christ in every aspect of life.

True Christianity is not confined to a specific religious label or cultural identity. It is a way of life that reflects the mind of Christ and the will of God. As Paul writes, *"I have been crucified with Christ, and I no longer live, but Christ lives in me"* (Galatians 2:20, NIV). This profound truth reveals that Christianity is not about us but about Christ living through us.

Christianity beyond Religion

Christianity is often misunderstood as just another religion, but it is fundamentally different. While religions focus on rituals, rules, and external practices, Christianity is about a transformative relationship with Christ. Jesus demonstrated this by living a life that transcended cultural and religious boundaries.

For example, Jesus was circumcised and observed Jewish customs (Luke 2:21), yet He consistently challenged traditions that contradicted God's will. At age twelve, He declared, *"Didn't you know I had to be in my Father's house?"* (Luke 2:49, NIV), showing His primary allegiance to God, not human traditions.

Jesus' interactions with outcasts, such as the Samaritan woman (John 4:7-29), further illustrates that true Christianity is inclusive and compassionate. It does not discriminate based on race, religion, or social status. Instead, it seeks to restore life and bring hope to all people.

The Essence of True Christianity

True Christianity is characterized by unconditional love, humility, and a commitment to God's will. God's work is prioritized ahead of one's profession or any other interest. True Christianity is not about seeking recognition or competing with other faiths but about reflecting Christ's love in a broken world. There are three fundamental principles that define a true Christian:

1. Unconditional Love

Jesus taught that the greatest commandment is to love God and love others (Matthew 22:37-39). This love is not selective or conditional but extends even to enemies (Matthew 5:44). True Christians are peacemakers, embodying God's love in their actions and attitudes (Matthew 5:9).

2. Humility and Servant-hood

True Christianity is marked by humility and a servant's heart. Jesus washed His disciples' feet, demonstrating that greatness in God's Kingdom is measured by service, not status (John 13:12-17). Paul echoed this principle, urging believers to *"do nothing out of selfish ambition or vain conceit, but in humility consider others better than yourselves"* (Philippians 2:3, NIV).

3. Faith of Jesus, as opposed to Faith in Jesus

There is a crucial distinction between having faith *in* Jesus and upholding the faith *of* Jesus. Faith in Jesus acknowledges His identity and work, but the faith of Jesus involves living as He lived—trusting God completely, obeying

145

His will, and loving sacrificially. True Christians are not merely believers; they are followers, embodying Christ's faith in their daily lives.

The Challenge of True Christianity

Living as a true Christian is not easy. Jesus warned that the path to eternal life is narrow and difficult (Matthew 7:13-14). It requires surrendering one's will, resisting conformity to worldly values, and enduring opposition. Living a new life in Christianity demands forsaking the physical responsibilities of this world, as one is no longer of this world. It is often impossible for those with whom one coexists to accept one's transformed life.

1. Resisting Conformity

Jesus refused to conform to traditions that contradicted God's will. Similarly, true Christians must resist the pressure to conform to cultural or religious norms that conflict with God's principles. This often leads to misunderstanding and persecution, but it is the cost of discipleship (John 15:18-20). A person may be rejected by those considered closest to them, but rather than feeling uncomfortable, they feel happier, as that treatment signifies being God's child.

2. Avoiding Idolatry

Idolatry is not limited to worshiping physical objects; it can also involve idolizing leaders, miracles, or material success. Jesus warned against such distractions, emphasizing that true worship is in spirit and truth (John 4:23-24). True Christians focus on their relationship with God, not on external signs or human accolades.

3. Embracing Persecution

Persecution is an inevitable part of the Christian journey. Jesus assured His followers, "Everyone who wants to live a godly life in Christ Jesus will be persecuted" (2 Timothy 3:12, NIV). True Christians endure opposition with grace, knowing that their ultimate reward is in heaven (Matthew 5:11-12).

The Mark of a True Christian

The defining mark of a true Christian is love. Jesus said, "By this everyone will know that you are my disciples, if you love one another" (John 13:35, NIV). This love is not superficial or selective but reflects the selfless, sacrificial love of Christ.

1. Love in Action

True Christianity is not about words but actions. It is about feeding the hungry, clothing the naked, and visiting the imprisoned (Matthew 25:35-40). It is about forgiving those who wrong us and praying for those who persecute us (Matthew 5:44).

2. Unity in Diversity

True Christians celebrate diversity and promote unity. They recognize that all believers are part of one body, regardless of race, gender, or social status (Galatians 3:28). They focus on what unites them—faith in Christ—rather than what divides them.

3. Joy in Suffering

True Christians find joy even in suffering, knowing that their trials refine their faith and bring glory to God (James 1:2-4). They live with an eternal perspective, trusting that their present struggles are temporary compared to the glory that awaits them (Romans 8:18).

The New Civilization

True Christianity ushers in a new civilization—a restoration of the harmony between humanity and God that was lost in Eden. It is a way of life characterized by love, humility, and obedience to God's will.

As Paul writes, *"You were taught, with regard to your former way of life, to put off your old self, which is being corrupted by its deceitful desires; to be made new in the attitude of your minds; and to put on the new self, created to be like God in true righteousness and holiness"* (Ephesians 4:22-24, NIV).

True Christianity is not about external practices or religious labels but about living in alignment with God's will. It is about embodying the love, humility, and faith of Christ in a world that often opposes His values.

As we strive to live as true Christians, let us remember that our ultimate goal is not to be celebrated by the world but to glorify God. May we reflect His love, endure persecution with grace, and live as ambassadors of His Kingdom.

CHAPTER 30

THE SIGNIFICANCE OF THE GREAT COMMISSION

All Christians bear the responsibility of fulfilling the Great Commission. The privilege of accessing the life-giving truth of the gospel comes with the duty to share it with others.

To withhold this invaluable information is not merely an oversight—it is a grave failure of stewardship. It is akin to receiving a sum of money on behalf of a community, only to hoard it for personal gain.

Such behaviour is not just selfish; it borders on criminal negligence. The gospel, designed to benefit all humanity, must flow freely and without hindrance. The Great Commission was entrusted to the eleven apostles, but its scope extends far beyond them.

The gospel's transformative power was meant to transcend boundaries—cultural, geographical, and temporal. Yet, today, many who claim to follow Christ fail to share the message of salvation with those around them.

This reluctance is a sin of omission, rooted in self-centeredness rather than the selfless love Christ exemplified. The stakes are high: the spiritual survival of others is intertwined with our own obedience to Christ's command.

It is better never to have received the gospel than to receive it and keep it to oneself. The principles of God's Kingdom are universal, addressing the deepest needs of humanity. When we fail to share these truths, we contribute to the perpetuation of evil in the world.

Jesus declared Himself the light of the world (John 1:9), and He commissioned His followers to be that light as well (Matthew 5:14). Yet, looking at the state of the world, it is evident that many Christians have neglected this sacred duty.

The failure to fulfil the Great Commission is a serious issue, and its root causes must be identified and addressed. In my view, two major obstacles stand in the way: authoritarianism and human traditions. These twin pillars of resistance stifle the free flow of the gospel and hinder its transformative power.

Authoritarianism: A Modern-Day Pharisees

Authoritarianism in the church mirrors the hypocrisy of the scribes and Pharisees in Jesus' time. Jesus rebuked them sharply:

"Woe to you, scribes and Pharisees, hypocrites! For you shut the kingdom of heaven in people's faces. For you neither enter yourselves nor allow those who would enter to go in" (Matthew 23:13, ESV).

Tragically, this same spirit persists today among some Christian leaders. They wield authority not to serve, but to control, effectively blocking others from entering God's Kingdom. These leaders may have good intentions, but their obsession with power and self-importance blinds them to the true mission of the church.

They create hierarchies that exclude rather than include, and they prioritize institutional preservation over the spread of the gospel. This authoritarian culture is a direct contradiction to the servant leadership modelled by Jesus.

The Stranglehold of Tradition

Human traditions, while often well-meaning, can become barriers to the gospel. Traditions provide a sense of identity and continuity, but they can also stifle innovation and discourage individual initiative.

In many churches, customs and rituals take precedence over the transformative power of the Holy Spirit. Leaders cling to outdated practices, refusing to adapt even when change could lead to greater effectiveness in fulfilling the Great Commission.

Jesus confronted this issue head-on: *"You have let go of the commands of God and are holding on to human traditions"* (Mark 7:8, NIV). Traditions, whether national, tribal, or denominational, often become idols that distract from the core mission of the church. They create a false sense of security, leading believers to rely on rituals rather than a living relationship with Christ.

The Power of Individual Responsibility

The Great Commission is not the exclusive domain of pastors, theologians, or church leaders. It is the responsibility of every believer. Each Christian has a unique testimony and a personal understanding of Christ's teachings. When we allow authoritarianism and tradition to silence us, we rob the world of the diverse ways in which God's truth can be shared.

Imagine the impact if every Christian spoke boldly about the value of Jesus, unencumbered by fear or institutional constraints. The gospel would spread like wildfire, transforming lives and communities overnight. Yet, this vision is often thwarted by those who resist change and cling to power. Authoritarians and traditionalists alike vilify those who challenge the status quo, labelling them as divisive or rebellious.

A Call to Action

Despite these challenges, there is hope. The work of the Holy Spirit cannot be contained by human structures or traditions. As one anonymous supporter of this ministry reminded me, *"We will prevail in the end."* This assurance is a reminder that we are not alone in this mission. Countless believers are praying, working, and striving to fulfil the Great Commission in their own contexts.

The church is not a hierarchy but a body, with each member playing a vital role. Just as a football team relies on every player to achieve victory, the church depends on the collective effort of all believers. However, unlike in sports, where individual stars are celebrated, in the church, all glory belongs to Christ. He is the one who empowers and enables us to fulfil His mission.

Conclusion: The Spirit Leads, Not Traditions or Authorities

The Great Commission is not about human authority or institutional power. It is about the free flow of the Holy Spirit, working through every believer to spread the message of Jesus. Authoritarianism and tradition must not be allowed to obstruct this divine mission. The Bible has been distributed worldwide, but its message must be lived and proclaimed by those who have experienced its transformative power.

As we move forward, let us remember that the battle is not ours alone. The Holy Spirit is our guide and our strength. We must resist the temptation to rely on human leaders or traditions and instead trust in the Spirit's leading. Together, as a united body of believers, we can fulfil the Great Commission and bring light to a world in desperate need of hope.

CHAPTER 31

EXPLORING THE CONCEPT
OF THE TRINITY

In Christianity, the doctrine of the Trinity stands as one of the most profound and debated theological concepts. While it is universally acknowledged in orthodox Christianity, its foundation in Scripture is often inferred rather than explicitly stated by Jesus Himself.

Since Jesus is the ultimate authority in Christian doctrine, His teachings must serve as the primary basis for validating any theological principle. The doctrine of the Trinity, though widely accepted, requires careful examination to determine its alignment with Jesus' explicit instructions and the broader biblical narrative.

The Great Commission and the Implied Trinity

The concept of the Trinity is often linked to Jesus' final instructions to His disciples before His ascension:

"All authority has been given to Me in heaven and on earth. Go therefore and make disciples of all the nations, baptizing them in the name of the Father and of the Son and of the Holy Spirit, teaching them to observe all things that I have commanded you; and lo, I am with you always, even to the end of the age" (Matthew 28:18-20, NKJV).

This passage is frequently cited as evidence of the Trinity, as it mentions the Father, Son, and the Holy Spirit in a unified context. However, it is important to note that Jesus does not explicitly define the Trinity here.

Instead, He emphasizes the authority given to Him and the disciples' mission to baptize and teach. The mention of the Father, Son, and the Holy Spirit suggests a relational unity but does not provide a detailed theological framework for the Trinity as later developed by the Church.

Baptism and Spiritual Transformation

Baptism in the name of the Father, Son, and the Holy Spirit signifies a profound spiritual transformation. It represents an individual's entry into a new relationship with God, marked by faith in the gospel and obedience to Jesus' teachings. The apostle Peter draws a parallel between baptism and Noah's deliverance through water, highlighting its significance as a symbol of salvation and renewal:

"There is also an antitype which now saves us—baptism (not the removal of the filth of the flesh, but the answer of a good conscience toward God), through the resurrection of Jesus Christ" (1 Peter 3:21, NKJV).

Baptism, therefore, is not merely a ritual but a spiritual act that unites believers with the life, death, and resurrection of Jesus. It signifies a transition from a state of spiritual separation to one of communion with God.

However, this does not necessarily affirm the doctrine of the Trinity as traditionally understood. Instead, it underscores the transformative power of faith and obedience to Christ.

Jesus' Relationship with the Father and the Spirit

In His teachings, Jesus frequently spoke of His unique relationship with the Father, but excluding the Holy Spirit. He, however, assured His disciples that He would not leave them as orphans but would send the Holy Spirit to guide and comfort them:

"I will not leave you orphans; I will come to you. A little while longer and the world will see Me no more, but you will see Me. Because I live, you will live also. On that day you will know that I

am in My Father, and you in Me, and I in you" (John 14:18-20, NKJV).

Here, Jesus speaks of a profound spiritual unity between Himself, the Father, and His followers. He then introduces the Holy Spirit as the means by which this unity is realized. Moreover, Jesus describes the unity between the Father, Himself and the person concerned.

The communication does not suggest a triune God in the sense of three distinct persons co-equal in essence. Rather, it emphasizes the relational and functional unity between the Father, Son, where the Holy Spirit facilitates that unity in the work of redemption.

The Nature of the Holy Spirit

The Holy Spirit is often misunderstood as a separate, personified entity within the Trinity. However, Scripture describes the Holy Spirit as the presence and power of God at work in the world and in the lives of believers. The Oxford English Dictionary defines "spirit" as "the non-physical part of a person that is the seat of emotions and character; loosely translated as the soul."

In a biblical context, the Holy Spirit represents the pure and undefiled presence of God, which restores humanity to its original state of spiritual purity. Jesus warned against blaspheming the Holy Spirit, emphasizing its sacred nature:

"Anyone who speaks a word against the Son of Man, it will be forgiven him; but whoever speaks against the Holy Spirit, it will not be forgiven him, either in this age or in the age to come" (Matthew 12:32, NKJV).

This warning underscores the holiness of the Spirit qualifying God's nature and its role in renewing and transforming believers. The Holy Spirit is not a separate being but the very presence of God, enabling believers to live in accordance with His will.

Challenges to the Trinitarian Doctrine

The doctrine of the Trinity, as formulated by early Church councils, faces several challenges when examined through the lens of Scripture and logic:

Theological Speculation: The Trinity is a product of theological speculation, developed centuries after Jesus' ministry. While it seeks to explain the relationship between the Father, Son, and the Holy Spirit, it often relies on philosophical concepts rather than explicit biblical teaching.

Authoritarian Culture: The development of the Trinity was influenced by an authoritarian culture within the early Church, where certain leaders were deemed authoritative on matters of doctrine. This culture often stifled dissenting voices and marginalized those who questioned established teachings.

Majority Consensus: The doctrine of the Trinity was affirmed by a majority vote at earlier councils such as Nicaea and Constantinople. However, truth is not determined by democratic processes but alignment with Scripture and Jesus' teachings.

A Call to Re-examine the Trinity

The doctrine of the Trinity, while widely accepted, requires careful re-examination in light of Scripture. Jesus' teachings emphasize the unity of the Father, Son, and the Holy Spirit in the work of redemption, but they do not provide a detailed framework for the Trinity as later developed by the Church.

As believers, we are called to prioritize the teachings of Jesus and the biblical narrative over human traditions and theological speculations. In conclusion, the concept of the Trinity serves as a reminder of the profound mystery of God's nature and His work in the world.

However, it is essential to approach this doctrine with humility and a commitment to biblical truth, recognizing that our understanding is limited and subject to refinement. By focusing on the relational unity between the Father, Son, and the Holy Spirit, we can better appreciate the transformative power of the gospel and the call to live in obedience to Christ.

Jesus expressed honour to His Father and also instructed His disciples to pray to the Father, without any mention of the Holy Spirit, in that process.

Those qualifying to become God's Children are reconciled with the Father, where Jesus is their brother. The only convincing role of the Holy Spirit is that of empowering us to understand the mysteries of God's Kingdom.

The Holy Spirit offers a unique perspective that helps clarify potential misunderstandings involving the Trinity, when contrasted with the human spirit. Job 32:8 mentions the presence of the spirit that defines the real person that Jesus died for. The spirit in man, being the seat of his emotion, is distinct from the Holy Spirit. This distinction does not suggest that the human spirit is a separate entity from the individual.

The primary difference between the human spirit and the Holy Spirit lies in their nature: the human spirit, while describing the man, is flawed, yet the Holy Spirit is pure and embodies God's essence. The human spirit encompasses both good and evil, whereas the Holy Spirit is flawless. Importantly, neither the Holy Spirit nor the human spirit can be measured or quantified in physical terms.

CHAPTER 32

THE BROTHERHOOD OF
HUMANITY

I n a world filled with ornamental objects, nothing compares to the beauty of humanity. Yet, I have known men and women with stunning physical appearances whose actions were as evil as Satan's. Conversely, I have encountered individuals whose outward appearance was far from appealing, yet their character was as kind and accommodating as one could imagine.

This irony underscores the complexity of human existence. Life feels empty without understanding its true purpose, and nothing is more vital than comprehending the essence of humanity.

The greatness of humanity lies not in judging others by their physical appearance but in recognizing their spiritual essence. Conflicts, wars, and brutal battles often stem from a failure to understand the principles of humanity.

The solution, however, is not as complicated as it may seem: it begins with recognizing Jesus as the cornerstone of understanding humanity. Falsehood, not truth, is the root of confusion and the incurable diseases plaguing humanity. True happiness can only be found when one discovers their purpose in existence.

Solving humanity's problems may appear unattainable, yet it can be as simple as understanding Jesus. The key is to move beyond the misconception that idolizing Jesus' personality is what matters, and instead focus on adopting His principles.

Rather than viewing Jesus solely as a member of the Trinity, we must strive to emulate His way of life. If we admire His actions, what prevents us from applying the same principles in our interactions with others? The outward appearance of humanity is insignificant compared to the inward spirit.

In John 1:29, Jesus is described as the Lamb who takes away the sin of humanity—not sins, but sin. This distinction is crucial. Jesus sacrificed Himself to redeem humanity from this inherent sin, which deserves identification and confrontation. All other unacceptable behaviours are merely symptoms of this singular sin. His followers are called to emulate His example, shaping themselves in His image.

However, confusion arises when people idolize the Lamb rather than understanding His mission. In this world, we are surrounded by both virtuous and wicked individuals. Only those who follow Jesus truly comprehend the nature of humanity, enabling them to guide others away from sin.

Jesus, as the Lamb of God, embodied the sinfulness of humanity without being sinful Himself. His followers are called to do the same—not by elevating themselves above others but by understanding and empathizing with those trapped in sin.

As the Apostle Paul demonstrated, this does not mean condoning sin but rather meeting people where they are to guide them toward redemption. In 1 Corinthians 9:19-21 (NKJV) Paul writes:

"Though I am free and belong to no one, I have made myself a slave to everyone, to win as many as possible. To the Jews I became like a Jew, to win the Jews. To those under the law, I became like one under the law (though I myself am not under the law), so as to win those under the law. To those not having the law I became like one not having the law (though I am not free from God's law but am under Christ's law), so as to win those not having the law."

Paul's approach was not about asserting superiority over others, but about sacrificially serving others. This is the essence of true Christianity—not appearing sinless among sinners but actively engaging with them to bring about transformation. This perspective also sheds light on the dichotomy between introverts and extroverts, which is essential for understanding the singular nature of humanity's sin.

An introvert is primarily focused on their own thoughts, feelings, and personal affairs, while an extrovert is outgoing, sociable, and concerned with the external affairs of others. These two personality types are often so different that they struggle to coexist. Yet, both introverts and extroverts can be entangled in sin.

However, Jesus' teachings suggest that extroverts may have a greater chance of aligning with those on the right-hand side of the King at the time of resurrection and judgment of ordinary humanity (Matthew 25:32-46).

The individuals described in Matthew 25:34-46 are not necessarily those who have heard the gospel of Jesus. They are ordinary people judged on the last Great Day (Revelation 20:11-13). Their judgment is not based on their response to the gospel but on their actions toward others.

Humans do well when contributing to the welfare of their fellow men. This includes those who lived before Jesus and those who were never enlightened by His message.

Introverts and extroverts are defined by their distinct characteristics. Introverts tend to focus on themselves and are often seen as peaceful, while extroverts are more inclined to solve others' problems, as illustrated in the Parable of the Good Samaritan.

Interestingly, extroverts will be surprised when identified as righteous, just as introverts do not see themselves as evil. Neither personality type is inherently motivated by religion, but introverts may be more inclined to seek comfort in religious structures, while extroverts find joy in addressing others' needs.

Jesus stated, *"No one can come to Me unless the Father who sent Me draws them"* (John 6:44). This highlights the mixed nature of humanity—a blend of good and evil that will be meticulously sifted on the Day of Judgment.

As humans, we should strive to look beyond our own interests. Acting as a Good Samaritan, doing what is beneficial for others, is admirable. The golden rule—treat others as you would like to be treated—remains timeless.

The Good Samaritan was not necessarily religious; he was an extrovert compelled to help others in need. Introverts may benefit from cultivating a more extroverted mindset, while extroverts should continue their selfless conduct. The challenge lies in understanding the true significance of Jesus' gospel, as this is where deception often takes root.

Jesus said, *"Enter through the narrow gate. For wide is the gate and broad is the road that leads to destruction, and many enter through it. But small is the gate and narrow the road that leads to life, and only a few find it"* (Matthew 7:13-14).

Regrettably, few take Scripture seriously, as many are more influenced by personal interests than by the teachings of Jesus. This has led to the rise of denominationalism in modern Christianity, where introverts often find comfort in the security of like-minded believers.

True Christianity, however, transcends denominational boundaries. It is not about seeking comfort within a specific group but about being spiritually guided by the Holy Spirit. As Jesus told Peter, *"You will be led where you do not wish to go"* (John 21:18).

The same applies to all who genuinely follow Jesus. Christianity is not about conforming to denominational structures but about embracing a sacrificial commitment to humanity, guided by the Spirit.

CHAPTER 33

Deducing the Truth: A Path to Freedom

Human suffering, criminality, and societal dysfunction often stem from misinformation rather than deliberate malice. Misjudging others for their actions is itself a consequence of misunderstanding the root causes of their behaviour.

This insight sheds light on the mystery of Jesus' sacrifice—He chose redemption over condemnation, emphasizing the transformative power of truth over punishment. Sin and falsehood create a world of chaos, where misinformation spreads easily, leading to destruction.

As the Scripture says:
"My people are destroyed for lack of knowledge. Because you have rejected knowledge, I also will reject you from being priest for Me; because you have forgotten the law of your God, I also will forget your children" (Hosea 4:6 NKJV).

Jesus provided a clear path from confusion to freedom, warning against the dangers of following falsehoods. To those who believed in Him, He said:

"If you abide in My word, you are My disciples indeed. And you shall know the truth, and the truth shall make you free" (John 8:31-32 NKJV).

This principle is akin to following a user manual for a product. Just as a prudent user adheres to instructions to avoid malfunction, humanity must heed divine guidance to avoid self-destruction. Yet, many ignore these basic principles, learning instead through painful experiences. This article explores strategies for escaping confusion and aligning with truth.

The Allure of Misinformation

In today's world, information is often judged by its packaging—eloquent speech, impressive credentials, or physical appearance. Advertisements, for instance, rely on captivating visuals and emotional appeals to sell products. However, truth is not always found in what is outwardly attractive or emotionally overwhelming. A biblical example portraying God's communication with the Prophet Elijah illustrates this:

"The Lord said, 'Go out and stand on the mountain in the presence of the Lord, for the Lord is about to pass by.' Then a great and powerful wind tore the mountains apart and shattered the rocks, but the Lord was not in the wind. After the wind, there was an earthquake, but the Lord was not in the earthquake. After the earthquake came a fire, but the Lord was not in the fire. And after the fire came, a gentle whisper" (1 Kings 19:11-12 NKJV).

This "gentle whisper" represents the inner voice of conscience, a divine guide within every individual. Despite the noise of external influences, a person might receive; this quiet voice affirms or challenges our choices. Ignoring it often leads to poor decisions and societal dysfunction. This reveals the cause of all problems bedevilling humanity.

The Role of Conscience in Society

Zimbabwe's economic and political challenges are often blamed on leaders, but the root cause lies deeper. Many citizens, swayed by charismatic politicians, ignore their inner voice. This form of idolatry—elevating human leaders above divine truth—leads to collective suffering.

Similarly, modern Christians often absolve themselves of responsibility, citing the world's inherent sinfulness. Yet, Jesus' promise—*"You will know the truth, and the truth will set you free"*— as shown in John 8:32, remains unfulfilled for those who prioritize charismatic voices over their conscience.

This issue extends beyond Zimbabwe. In the USA, for example, many self-proclaimed Christians support leaders like

Donald Trump, despite evidence of his divisive and harmful policies. Their allegiance often stems from a superficial understanding of Christianity, conflating it with political ideology, influenced by morality, rather than the teachings of Jesus.

Christianity: A Call to Love, Not Condemn

Christianity is not about condemning sinners but about embodying Jesus' love and truth. Jesus welcomed sinners like Zacchaeus, helping them discover their worth and turn from sin (Luke 19:1-10). He reserved His harshest criticism for the self-righteous Pharisees, who judged others while ignoring their own flaws. Modern Christianity often strays from Jesus' model, persuaded by feelings.

Many focus on condemning behaviours like abortion or homosexuality, mistaking morality for the essence of Jesus' message. While Jesus never demanded moral perfection; He offered grace and transformation to those engrossed in sin. True Christianity liberates individuals from confusion by guiding them to listen to their inner voice and embrace truth, found in every human.

The Danger of Charismatic Deception

Charismatic leaders, whether in politics or religion, often exploit their followers' desire for certainty and belonging. In Zimbabwe, the Chitepo School of ideological indoctrination exemplifies this phenomenon.

Similarly, in the USA, Trump's supporters appear loyal to him as a personality figure, despite his divisive actions. This loyalty causes prioritizing charisma over truth. The challenge remains in engaging those indoctrinated by charismatic figures.

Rational discourse often fails to reach their inner feelings, deeply entrenched, but not confronted. Breaking this cycle requires a return to the gentle whisper of conscience, which transcends external influences. Otherwise, the person remains deluded.

The Path to Freedom

Freedom begins with embracing Jesus' foundation of truth. Even without explicit knowledge of Scripture, individuals can access truth through their conscience, as demonstrated by the Good Samaritan (Luke 10:25-37). This innate goodness reflects God's image in humanity, affirming His decision to sacrifice His Son for our redemption. Jesus' actions are not associated with making Himself great.

Christians are called to embody Jesus by sacrificing their interests for others, rather than avoiding or condemning them. Pretending to represent Jesus while acting contrary to His teachings is the ultimate betrayal of faith and should be regarded as worse than other sins.

Conclusion: Truth as the Foundation of Life

In a world of confusion, truth is often overshadowed by attractive but deceptive narratives. Wealth, power, and popularity can distract from the gentle whisper of conscience. Yet, as Jesus taught, the true treasure lies in aligning with divine truth as outlined in (Matthew 6:19-24).

By listening to our inner voice and embracing Jesus' teachings, we can escape confusion and contribute to a more just and compassionate world.

The United States, as a global leader, exemplifies the consequences of ignoring this principle. Its actions reverberate worldwide, making it imperative for its citizens to model truth and integrity.

Ultimately, the principle of deducing the truth is not just a personal endeavour but a collective responsibility to create a liveable world for all. Each person ought to listen to his or her inner conscience when reaching out to others.

CHAPTER 34

LIKE JESUS, EVERY INDIVIDUAL IS BORN WITH A MISSION

The arrival of Jesus in this world was a profound mystery, revealing the true significance of humanity. In a world filled with wonders, the greatest miracle of all is humanity itself. Every human being is a unique and incomparable creation, a living testament to God's divine craftsmanship.

While Jesus' life stands as an unparalleled miracle, His presence also serves to illuminate humanity's true identity as children of God. The mere thought of being called God's child should awaken awe and wonder, stirring the depths of our imagination. Yet, humanity's rejection of Jesus reflects a deeper tragedy: the rejection of God Himself.

Created in God's image, humans often turn away from their Creator and, in doing so, turn away from one another. Preaching Jesus means understanding that He came to reveal our true identity—not as children of a surrogate father, but as sons and daughters of God.

This shift in identity, from our earthly ties to our divine inheritance, is the greatest mystery of all. Many Christians today romanticize the idea of walking with Jesus during His time on earth, imagining the glory of witnessing His miracles firsthand.

Yet, they often overlook the profound truth that Jesus continues to interact with humanity through those who have embraced their identity as God's children. Modern Christianity sometimes idolizes a distant, unknown Jesus, but this perspective changes entirely when we realize that Jesus is present in every believer baptized in the name of the Trinity.

Jesus Himself promised His disciples, "I will not leave you as orphans; I will come to you. Before long, the world will not see me anymore, but you will see me. Because I live, you also will live" (John 14:18-19 NKJV).

Just as the world failed to recognize Jesus as God's Son during His earthly ministry, it remains blind to His presence among His followers today. True Christians are those who resonate with Jesus in every aspect of their lives, embodying His teachings and reflecting His love.

The Mission of Faith and Courage

The world is entangled in sin, and Jesus came to offer a way out of this labyrinth of confusion. He declared that those with faith as small as a mustard seed would perform even greater miracles than He did (John 14:12). This statement underscores the profound truth that there is no distinction between Jesus and those filled with the Holy Spirit.

Yet, many Christians struggle to attain the faith necessary to confront life's challenges. Why is this so? At the heart of this struggle lies cowardice, often fuelled by pride. Pride intimidates and suppresses, preventing individuals from stepping into their God-given potential.

Christians, however, are called to rise above fear, empowered by the Holy Spirit. For believers, death holds no sting, and danger is no deterrent when standing for the truth. Jesus exemplified this courage by enduring the cross, and He calls His followers to do the same:

"Whoever wants to be my disciple must deny themselves and take up their cross and follow me" (Matthew 16:24 NKJV).

This call to self-denial and sacrifice is the essence of Christianity. Yet, it is often overlooked or deliberately avoided, especially in a world where deception runs rampant.

Jesus warned of the dangers of wealth, stating, *"You cannot serve both God and money"* (Matthew 6:24). The Apostle Paul echoed this warning in his letter to Timothy, describing the love of money as *"a root of all kinds of evil"* (1 Timothy 6:10).

The Danger of Deception

Deception in Christianity often stems from a misplaced focus on hierarchy and authority. Many leaders elevate themselves, creating structures that prioritize their comfort and control over the equality Jesus taught. In doing so, they turn Jesus into an object of worship rather than an example to emulate. This contradicts Jesus' explicit instruction: *"But you are not to be called 'Rabbi,' for you have one Teacher, and you are all brothers"* (Matthew 23:8 NKJV).

True worship, as Jesus explained, is conducted "in Spirit and in truth" (John 4:24). It transcends worldly rituals and hierarchies, emphasizing a direct relationship with God.

Paul further emphasized this unity in Christ, stating, *"There is neither Jew nor Gentile, neither slave nor free, nor is there male and female, for you are all one in Christ Jesus"* (Galatians 3:28 NKJV).

This unity is beautifully illustrated in the functioning of the body of Christ, where each member plays a unique role (1 Corinthians 12). Just as a musical ensemble harmonizes without one voice dominating, the Church thrives when each believer contributes their spiritual gifts in unity.

The fact that one member of the singing group may possess exceptional skills in coaching and coordinating others is not immediately apparent, except for the unified quality they collectively project.

The Call to Fulfil Our Purpose

Jesus fulfilled His mission through His death and resurrection, establishing God's Church and redeeming humanity from sin. Yet, a common misconception in modern Christianity is the belief that Jesus is separate from His followers. Jesus Himself identified with His disciples, saying, *"Whatever you did for one of the least of these brothers and sisters of mine, you did for me"* (Matthew 25:40 NKJV).

Every individual born into this world has the potential to become a child of God by following Jesus' teachings. Tragically, many live and die without realizing this purpose, ensnared by deception and distraction.

Jesus took on the responsibility of redeeming humanity, and those who are enlightened are called to make similar sacrifices. Losing one's life in service to God is the highest honour, a testament to the transformative power of faith.

In the end, the mission of every individual mirrors that of Jesus: to reveal the glory of God through a life of faith, courage, and selfless love. By embracing our identity as God's children and living in harmony with His will, we fulfil the purpose for which we were born.

The call is to emulate Jesus, rather than distance oneself, assuming the calling is solely for worship.

CHAPTER 35

THE MOST PERILOUS RISK IN CHRISTIANITY

H ave you ever considered a shepherd who abandons ninety-nine sheep, leaving them vulnerable to wolves, in pursuit of one that is lost? Why endanger so many for the sake of one? At first glance, it seems illogical, but a deeper understanding reveals otherwise.

Jesus was not merely sharing a pleasant tale; He was unveiling a harmful mindset that continues to plague Christians today. Some interpret this parable to justify their arrogance rather than grasp its true meaning, which conveys the opposite. The narrative is presented in four parts to assist the reader, who may feel numb and perplexed by this exposition.

Part 1: The Parable That Confuses People

In Luke 15:1-7, Jesus tells this story after the religious leaders (Pharisees) complain that He's spending time with "sinners." They think they're already holy enough and look down on others. They assume that they are in the fold and do not need repentance, unlike those considered to be the degraded sinners. In His teaching, Jesus flips the script:

The Lost Sheep = The sinner who knows they're broken and needs God, attracting God's mercy, thereby assured of receiving salvation.
The Ninety-Nine = The considered "good religious people" comfortably assuming they don't need repentance, as meticulously keeping the requirements of the Law.

The shocking aspect is that the shepherd leaves the ninety-nine to find the one in appalling conditions. Why? The ninety-nine believe they are safe, but their pride is actually more dangerous than the lost sheep's sinfulness. Therefore, the shepherd did not hesitate to leave them at the mercy of the ravenous wolves. Jesus used the same parable when addressing those who took comfort in being His disciples rather than maintaining humility.

In Luke 15:1-7, Jesus addressed the Pharisees and scribes, who were religious but not His disciples. The Pharisees were not considered part of His fold. The confusion regarding this parable arises in Matthew 18:10-14, where Jesus speaks to the disciples.

It should be clearly understood that the significance of the parable was intended to warn the complacent, akin to the message directed at the Pharisees and scribes. The shepherd illustrates the preference of rescuing the lost sinner over the ninety-nine, mistakenly viewed as safe.

Part 2: The Trap of "I'm already Good Enough"

The Pharisees believed they were righteous because they followed religious rules. But Jesus told one of their leaders, Nicodemus: *"Unless someone is born again, they cannot see God's Kingdom"* (John 3:3)

Nevertheless, the same erroneous assumption befell the disciples, whose problem manifested in their disputes regarding seniority. They exhibited a complacent attitude similar to that of the Pharisees and Scribes. They did not comprehend the significance of Christianity, just as most people today remain oblivious to what Christianity truly implies, which intrinsically requires the awareness of the fact that:

No one is inherently righteous before God—not even churchgoers. If there were even one person worthy of being considered good, Jesus' sacrifice on the cross would have been unnecessary. This truth is unknown to many.

Self-righteousness is dangerous, the belief that "I am better than those sinners," is a greater problem than the sins of the "lost." The more aware a person is of their need for salvation, the better off they would be. The worst sinner is the one who assumes they are good in God's eyes. This is the greatest irony of Christianity.

171

The ninety-nine sheep were not truly safe—they were even in more danger because they did not realize they needed the Shepherd just as much as the lost one. Jesus uses the parable to convey this reality to those with ears.

The aspect of hearing but not understanding was designed that way for ordinary people. This was the main reason for Him teaching in parables. His use of parables to project this truth reflects the core essence that led to His coming and Christianity.

.Part 3: A Warning to Christians Today

The same parable becomes more terrifying when directed at His disciples (Matthew 18:10-14). Jesus said this Parable with hindsight of how it would affect Christians of our time. *"Woe to the world because of the things that cause people to stumble! Such things must come, but woe to the person through whom they come!"* (Matthew 18:7). The amplification of this impact is confirmed in the following sentiment:

"If anyone causes one of these little ones who believe in Me to sin, it would be better for them to have a millstone hung around their neck and be drowned in the sea" (Matthew 18:6)
Why such an extreme warning? Because:

Leading believers astray is worse than being a "lost sinner."

A sinner can still repent. But someone who corrupts others (like false teachers) is like a poison spreading in the church. Nothing can be considered more dangerous than assuming the sole responsibility of Jesus, yet existing in the flesh, which embodies sinfulness.

It's the "unforgivable sin."

Jesus stated that all sins can be forgiven except for the sin of blasphemy against the Holy Spirit (Matthew 12:31-32). Rejecting God's truth while claiming to represent Him can be perilously aligned with the devil, as it also leads to destruction (Hebrews 10:26-27).

The Scribes and Pharisees, although viewed negatively in Jesus' time, were not in a worse condition than those of today. Hence, Jesus protected the Pharisees by teaching in parables. This is where the image of a millstone around someone's neck becomes relevant. Imagine how impossible it would be for a person with a millstone hung around their neck to avoid sinking.

The severity of causing one who has attained the status of being God's child to stumble is considered incomparable to any other sin. The person led astray is irretrievable. Thus, the folly of misleading others while presuming to be more knowledgeable is extremely perilous.

Part 4: None can be "Too Good" to need Jesus.

If you think, *"I go to church, I tithe, I'm a good person— I don't need to change,"* you might be one of the "ninety-nine." But more so, you could be the candidate of someone poised to have a millstone on the neck; when assuming leadership over others.

Humility is the key—always recognizing our need for God. Accepting the condition of Christianity implies understanding that there cannot be anything more humiliating than the commitment to Christianity.

Beware of False Leaders

Jesus warned about *"wolves in sheep's clothing"* (Matthew 7:15). Another way of spotting such people is by their assumption of authority over others in Christianity. A true spiritual leader points people to Christ, not to themselves.

Forgiveness over Judgment

Jesus taught that we must forgive others *"seventy times seven"* (Matthew 18:22) because we *all* fail. The principle of forgiving others always and being willing to change when proven wrong helps in keeping focused.

The only damning sin is pride—refusing to recognize that we all need grace, without exception. Understanding Godly principle does not make anyone greater, but requires sacrificing for those still in darkness.

Final Thought: The Real Message of the Lost Sheep

The parable isn't really about the *one* sheep—it's about the *ninety-nine* who *think* they're fine. Jesus is saying: *"It is not the healthy who need a doctor, but the sick. I have not come to call the righteous, but sinners to repentance"* (Luke 5:31-32)

So the question those reading this should be: Are you humble enough to admit you still need the Shepherd? Or do you think you're already one of the "safe" ninety-nine?

Why This Matters Today

Complacency led to the downfall of the Roman Empire, as they assumed superiority over the Barbarians, only to be defeated by them. Many churches today focus on appearances, such as large congregations, wealth, and strict rules, but neglect the essence of Jesus' teachings. This keeps them ensconced in the ninety-nine bracket.

True Christianity is not about outward holiness but recognizing our brokenness and relying on God's mercy daily. When allowed to serve, we should do so selflessly, without expecting any reward from those of this world.

GLOSSARY

Altruism: Selfless concern for the well-being of fellow humans, at one's own expense, when taking full responsibility in addressing issues that are beneficial to everyone.

Anyone accepting Christ will never see death (John 8:51): While Christians hold eternal value, what is real to non-Christians ends at the point of their deaths. At the resurrection, the wicked become estranged from the then-current realities. Resurrected Christians, including Patriarch Abraham share in fulfilled hope with the surviving Christians.

Christian: God's Child, living by Godly principles, not merely claiming membership to some church organization, but led by The Holy Spirit, in grace and humility.

Christianity: The practice of the Christian faith––not necessarily as another religion of this world, or as commonly understood in our modern-day Christian world.

Church: A spiritual entity, or organism founded by Christ, (Matt. 16:18), without a physical structure, as ordinarily observable, comprising those yielding to God's Spirit. This disregards a denomination to which the person belongs or subscribes.

Civilization: Human society with social structures, influencing the behaviour of humanity when pursuing survival objectives. The conditions are currently self-centred, as originating from Adam. The New Civilization advocates altruism ahead of self-centeredness.

Confusion: Misunderstanding, when mixing up goodness with evil. Making what is good evil and what is evil good. In its advanced degree, confusion describes insanity. The opposite of confusion is, therefore, order.

Creation: The process of producing something out of nothing. Everything existing is a product of God's creation. Humans were fashioned with creative minds, but currently, they are mostly the opposite of what they were created to be.

Death: Departure of life, as perceived in earthly organisms, either sustained by flesh and blood or any other organic condition, such as in plants.

Deliverance: The process of being salvaged from bondage, taking advantage of Jesus' grace. The physical body, composed of flesh, provides prison-hood for humanity, created in God's image, needing deliverance through Christ's works.

Disciples: Christ's followers, before being filled with The Holy Spirit, after which they become God's children––sharing Godly principles––no longer regarded as mere disciples.

Faith: Being sure of what is hoped for and certain of what is not seen (Heb. 11:1)––achievable through submission to Christ in the Spirit. Devising own programmes of good works without Christ is not exercising faith.

Fellowship: Companionship of those converging to pursue shared interests, according to intended objectives–– influencing outsiders to join in––giving relief without discrimination.

Flesh: Soft substance, consisting of muscle tissue and fat, sustained by bones, with blood circulating, as the person or animal survives in energy, space and time, subject to dying.

Formation of Adam: In manipulating the dust of the earth, Adam was formed (Gen. 2:7). Compare this with the Man's creation (Gen. 1:26-27). Noticeably, Man in God's image, was produced from nothing, while Adam was formed from the dust of the ground.

Gnashing of teeth: A figurative term, describing a bad experience, undergone by most Christians, after having been rejected at Christ's second coming (Matt. 22:13-14).

God: The Supreme Being—outside time and space—with nothing existing without Him—as revealed in love, creation and through Christ. God's nature—being Spiritual—cannot be likened to anything physical (Exod. 20:4).

God's Image: The likeness of God—as being Spiritual—is also conferred on humanity—expected to give up their current physical nature (John 4:24, 1 Cor. 15:48-49, Genesis 1:26-27).

God's Kingdom: To be fully realized after Christ's millennial reign. However, true Christians are currently under God's Kingdom but will constitute God's Kingdom under Christ, at His Second coming (Rev. 20:4, Ps. 37:29, Matt. 5:5, 1 Cor. 6:2, Rev. 2:26, and Rev. 5:10). God's Kingdom does not consist of anything physical (Rev 21:1-5).

God's will: Manifesting in God's Love, righteousness and goodness is desirable for human survival. This is like a sea-voyager using a compass; a device containing a magnetized pointer, to the north and bearings from it. While to the voyager the compass serves as a guide in determining direction towards a desired destination, to Christians, God's will is the direction, when avoiding error towards death.

Gospel: This means Good News, which is the opposite of bad news—as disseminated through the public media. The gospel provides solutions toward the unmitigated hope of life; notwithstanding the past, present and possible future sins.

Grace: Free and unmerited favour or goodwill, offered to the entire humanity––which is different from known favours, bestowed as a reward for good works. Grace is the fundamental aspect of Christianity. Those taking advantage of grace, acknowledge the supremacy of Christ's ability to nullify past, present and possible future sins.

Heaven: The destination after pursuing altruism, in conformity with God's will, made possible by the power of The Holy Spirit. Heaven's price invites repudiating of a self-centred lifestyle when pursuing altruism, through Christ.

Hell: The unfavourable result of self-centeredness, possibly, as experienced in this life; but, as fully pronounced, to affect sinners at the final judgment. Humanity needs survival, yet the alluring fantasy of self-centeredness brings hell, in this life or at the Great White Throne Judgment (Rev. 20:12-15).

Holy Spirit: A component of Godly nature. The Holy Spirit accurately describes God's power among Christians—without which there is no Christianity. The Holy Spirit influences God-like behaviour—among those yielding to Christ—when having the Power of the Holy Spirit.

Humility: Viewing others as also important––when selflessly serving them––contributing towards programmes that improve their well-being ahead of one's physical welfare. A humble person values high achievements as relevant––only when others benefit.

Jesus Christ: The Being that is described in Isaiah 9:6. His physical appearance facilitated effective communication towards establishing altruism—leading to the ability to solve all riddles of human existence—when applying those principles. Humanity is expected to adopt the behaviour of Jesus Christ, to attain salvation.

Judeo-Christian Bible: The Christian Bible was originally adopted from Jewish scrolls, but later encompassed the narratives of Jesus' works. Its structure bears two divisions: the Old and New Testaments. The Old shows conditional pardon of sins, based on Moses' Law; while the New reveals the unconditional pardon of sins, based on Grace, through Jesus Christ.

[Glossary]

King of Kings and Lord of Lords: This describes the appearance of Jesus Christ and His saints, to be revealed at His Second Coming, before His designated millennial reign (Rev 19 & 20).

Life: That which cannot be measured or quantified, but animating material organisms. In humans and animal species, it provides intricate control of nerves, circulation of blood and the behaviour of body organs. In other species without blood, like plants, life causes germination, growth and multiplication. Life does not need a bodily form, yet bodily forms need life to survive. Jesus Christ represents Life (John 14:6).

Love: Interpreted loosely, is an intense feeling of deep affection, or deep romantic attachment to someone, or a great interest and pleasure in something. This describes affinity; as opposed to God's Love, which is unconditional.

Messiah: The promised deliverer, as prophesied in Hebrew Scriptures. Christians regard Jesus as The Messiah (Hebrew), "Christ" (Greek), "Deliverer" or "Redeemer" (English).

Miracle: An extraordinarily welcome, never anticipated event, attributed to a divine agency, inexplicable by natural or scientific laws. True Christians are not fascinated by miracles. One's existence is a greater miracle, when having become a true Christian.

Mystery: Something difficult or viewed as impossible to understand or explain. It is the secrecy or obscurity of something whose identity or nature is puzzling to ordinary humans. But encouraging the desire to understand--when obsessed with searching for knowledge and truth.

Order: The condition in which everything is arranged in rightful sequence, for desirable results. When brought to its advanced degree, order restores sanity. The opposite of order is confusion.

Personal salvation: Concern for self-benefit, emphasizing works, instead of grace to obtain salvation. It leads to pride, as the person puts standards that 'qualify' people in attaining salvation; instead of grace, regardless of sinful backgrounds.

Physical: The opposite of what is spiritual. Being matter—touched, felt, seen or visualised, as existing in matter, energy, space and time, but subject to perishing at some point in time. This includes humanity when existing in flesh and blood.

Prayer: A solemn petition—addressed to God for help—to overcome problems of physical nature and stress. Prayer appeals for divine intervention on believers who appreciate God's will, when facing challenges, in pursuit of physical survival.

Prayer without ceasing: Prayerfully maintaining God's will continuously, to remain in communion with the Spirit of God.

Pride: The aspect of valuing oneself as superior to others—attributed to Satan (Isa. 14:12-17 and Ezek. 28:13-17). A feeling of deep pleasure or satisfaction, derived from qualities, signifying past achievements, or possessions, leading to consciousness in feeling dignified.

Rabbi: Jewish term for Professor—wielding authority in knowledge—in any designated field. Christ took that position forever (Matt. 23:8). All humans are brothers and sisters. Those carrying superior data are equipped by Christ, who deserves all credit.

Real: What exists in fact—not imagined or supposed. Flesh, with its temporary attributes, is not real when compared with the spirit. *"So we fix our eyes not on what is seen, but on what is unseen. For what is seen is temporary, but what is unseen is eternal"* (2 Cor. 4:18 NIV).

Reconciliation: Overriding ministerial responsibility given to Christians—restoring relationships among peoples of diverse backgrounds and between humanity and God.

Redemption: The process of reclaiming ownership of what had previously been lost. To achieve this, Christ sacrificed His body through the cross to redeem humanity. Those who believe in Him are the ones privileged to benefit, as to receive the intended redemption.

Repentance: Changing from self-centeredness to altruism––when accepting Christ's teachings. After repentance, the person begins to appreciate helping others, rather than being helped.

Resurrection: The process of restoration to life after death. True Christians get resurrected celestially, at Christ's second coming. The rest of the dead get resurrected terrestrially––in their physical condition, after the millennium––with the possibility of a second death (Rev. 20:4-6, 12). The hope of resurrection is what sustains true Christianity.

Salvation: Realization of eternal life, through Christ, whose death and resurrection made salvation attainable. Salvation is possible for those still living, just as possible for dead sinners.

Satan: The wicked spirit-being, obsessed with opposing God's idea of redeeming humanity. Satan replaces grace with condemnation, Love is replaced with hatred, order is replaced with confusion and consequently, righteousness is replaced with evil. His power to manipulate is in ego—which he makes attractive to ordinary humanity.

Self-centeredness: Concern for promoting self, ahead of others, motivating the pride in humanity. The greatest shortcoming of self-centeredness is that it militates against those not subscribing to one's beliefs or practices—being what causes debilitating wars.

Sin: That which emanates from pride, leading to opposing everything Godly, hence adversary to human survival. All sins have been forgiven, through Christ, except the sin of pride.

Space: A viewpoint of dimension, as perceived by any individual, depending on background, seeing things differently, thereby making judgments differently.

Spirit: The non-physical component of humanity which is the seat of emotions and character. In manipulating the flesh, a person projects spiritual intention, either good or bad, through the physical nature. The term "Spirit" is divided into three: The Holy Spirit, typified in God. The spirit in Man, revealed in Job 32:8, as surrendered by Jesus at the cross (Luke 23:46) and the wicked spirit, typified in Satan.

Temple: In the Jewish faith and various other religions, a temple is God's sacred dwelling place (1 Kings 6:1-38). In Christianity, a temple is figurative, as represented in our physical bodies (1 Corinthians 3:16-17, 1 Corinthians 6:19–20, 2 Corinthians 6:16-18)

The devil: Another term for Satan, with ungodly schemes, which denote wickedness. The devil is accused of influencing humanity to behave badly.

Time: The method of gauging the duration of events in the physical sphere, though static. God, being outside time and space, knew about human existence, long before. Therefore, while time and space affect humanity, God is not affected.

Trinity: The doctrine of the Trinity is not explicitly revealed in scriptures, but adopted in theological studies. Trinity provides what appears logical to those attempting to solve God's identity, without the Holy Spirit. However, God cannot be likened to anything created, as He is the Creator. The riddle is solved when appreciating that Jesus is the way, the truth and the Life.

Universe: The physical universe comprises material things, existing in energy, space and time, as agreed, among physical humans. The spiritual universe implies one's own, as God spiritually communicates with individuals, depending on viewpoints.

[Glossary]

Value Addition: Enhancing improvement of other people's lives to reach their maximum potential, in health and education, ultimately leading to eternity.

BIBLIOGRAPHY

Bennett Roy: May 29, 2012, "Smoke and Mirrors: Another look at politics and ethnicity in Zimbabwe".
www.freezimbabwe.com

www.ingramcontent.com/pod-product-compliance
Lightning Source LLC
LaVergne TN
LVHW051119080426
835510LV00018B/2132